GOING
DEEPER

How the Inner Child
Impacts Your Sexual Addiction

EDDIE CAPPARUCCI, Ph.D., LPC

Copyright© 2023 by Eddie Capparucci

All rights reserved. No part of this book may be produced, stored in a retrieval system, or transmitted in any form or by any means without the publisher's prior written permission except by a reviewer who may quote brief passages in a review to be printed in a newspaper, magazine, or journal.

The author grants the final approval for this literary material.

ISBN: 9798866750993

PUBLISHED BY: Abundant Life Counseling, Highlands, NC

Printed in the USA. Suggested Retail Price (SRP) $22.95

© 2018 First Printing

© 2023 Second Printing

The cover photo is from an art project by Ukrainian artist Alexander Milov. Purchase his artwork at:

https://www.etsy.com/listing/1008144448/alexander-milov-love-sculpturedigital

The rights to all other photos used in this book were obtained through Dreamstime Images.

GOING DEEPER RESOURCES

Going Deeper Online Course

This 12-part video series will empower you by teaching you how to stay one step ahead of your Problematic Sexual Behaviors. It helps provide insights into managing your disorder and gives you the newfound capability to make healthy decisions. Conducted by Dr. Capparucci, you will go deeper in your recovery journey. You can learn more by visiting www.innerchild-sexaddiction.com

Going Deeper Clinician Training Program

An online training program is available for clinicians, coaches, and spiritual leaders who want to bring the Inner Child Model into their practice. The program is certified by Pure Life Academy, a division of Be Broken Ministries. Become certified in the Inner Child Model by visiting https://www.purelifeacademy.org/bundles/ictc

Going Deeper Workbook

This workbook is necessary for anyone who reads this book. The journal contains numerous exercises and is a companion to this book to assist you in gaining additional insights. Available at Amazon.

Going Deeper Community

Become a member of our Going Deeper Community, where members share what they are learning and serve to offer support to one another. This is a free community, and you can learn more by visiting https://goingdeeper.mn.co

DEDICATION

To my Lord and Savior Jesus Christ, who took a broken man and gave him purpose. He put me in a position where I could take the mistakes I made in the past and use them to assist in healing others in need. Never in my wildest dreams did I believe he would bless this ministry to the extent it has developed. I am blessed to be a prince of the King.

My wife Teri encouraged me to write when words were unavailable and to see new opportunities to assist those in need that I was overlooking. She instilled hope when I struggled through writer's block and has been a cornerstone in my life.

To my children, Chelsea, and Dakota, who have brought me much happiness and joy. I am so proud of the adults they have become.

To all the men who trusted me with their recovery and applied the principles, I believe will continue to assist them in successfully managing their PSBs. To their spouses who have worked hard to overcome the heartache and betrayal they have suffered at the hands of men they thought they could trust.

And to my faithful Labradors: Hunter and Bosco, who sat under my feet as I worked on this book's redrafting and new information. They have always been a great sense of comfort for me.

Finally, to my Inner Child, Little Eddie, who I am so grateful to come to know and, more importantly, who allowed me to experience the pain, disappointment, and heartache he endured as a child. While at times he can be a handful, he indeed is my friend.

What Clients Say About Their Inner Child

The following is feedback from a handful of clients in the initial stages of their Inner Child work describing the destructive nature and the negative impact the Inner Child has had in their lives.

Kevin, pornography addiction

"My Inner Child sits on the couch and looks out at the kids in the neighborhood playing. None of them knocked on my door to see if I wanted to join them. He feels left out. Now, if I feel left out when co-workers go to lunch but do not invite me, I want to hide and distract myself with porn, so I do not feel disappointed that no one cares. I can't take the thought of sitting on the couch and watching others enjoy themselves while I am dying inside."

Carmen, sexual and pornography addiction

"The kid is afraid. He's always been afraid. I can remember the constant bullying during elementary and middle school. I always looked forward to school breaks, including the summer, to escape the harassment. He is still that nervous kid who is always looking over his shoulder. Today, I struggle to trust new people I meet. He always thinks they are going to hurt us."

Charlie, pornography addiction

"My inner kid explodes when he hears someone being critical of me. And that sets off my anger. I hate being told I'm not good enough. I find myself exploding and looking at porn. When that happens, my kid quiets down. I have realized I am oversensitive to criticism, and my inner kid overreacts to comments that aren't meant to be critical. If I let him, he will lead me to continue to hurt my wife."

Terry, sexual addiction

"Abandonment is what causes my Inner Child to become fearful. Mom left my dad and brother when I was seven. She just ran away with another man, and we never saw her again. What mother leaves her children behind? If I start to feel someone is trying to distance themselves from me, I know my Inner Child is being activated, and I will soon start getting anxious. If I don't let myself become aware of what is happening, I will find myself at a strip club spending a ton of money on lap dances."

Bruce, pornography addiction

"Feeling like he is being controlled. That is what will get my little fella upset. He remembers mom was a control freak. Everything had to be done her way. I had no voice, and worst yet, all the things she made me do were with one goal in mind – making her look good. I have realized my Inner Child hates being told what to do. But I must let him know that often, what he believes is someone trying to control us is not always accurate. He sees all of them like mom."

Vic, sexual and pornography addiction

"During my recovery work, we originally thought boredom was the main trigger for my Inner Child. But with more self-reflection, we discovered it is all about lacking a sense of purpose. At 49 years old, I can't tell you what value I have in this life, and that makes my Inner Child incredibly sad. When my day-to-day life starts looking the same, he gets triggered, and I am left looking for an adrenaline rush, which I found for years with sex."

Alan, pornography addiction

"My Inner Child is very in tune whenever something occurs in which the message is being sent saying, 'I'm stupid.' And the person delivering that message most often is me. I was not fully aware of it until I started my therapy. Growing up with three older siblings, I was always laughed at whenever I made a mistake or said something that did not make sense. I cannot remember anyone calling me stupid, but I certainly felt that way. As an adult, if I made a mistake, I tried to shake it off, but later, I would see my mood shift, and I felt worthless. I then find myself heading off to watch porn. All the time, it was my Inner Child telling me how stupid we are."

Stan, same-sex attraction

"I have had a sex addiction for more years than I care to consider. I knew deep down that it was rooted in my childhood, but until I began my recovery work, I did not realize the extent and depth my childhood had on my addiction. Coming to understand the little boy inside me and coming to terms with many of the people who impacted me as a child has helped me turn my life around. I can now live by the terms of my adult self instead of the emotions of my little boy. He's still there and certainly has his moments, but his voice has become much softer, and his cries, not as loud."

WHAT CLINICIANS SAY ABOUT THE INNER CHILD MODEL™

"Any traditional, trauma-driven male sex or porn addict will easily find himself in the chapters of this enlightening look at how the Inner Child impacts sexual compulsivity. This is an excellent and necessary examination of the 'why' of sex and porn addiction, helpful primarily to men in sexual recovery who've established initial sobriety and need deeper, longer-term work to heal and remain sober."

—Robert Weiss, Ph.D., LCSW, author of Sex Addiction 101, Prodependence, and other books

"Going Deeper is about seeing your unwanted sexual behavior as a clarion call to heal the underlying heartaches in your story. A seasoned clinician, Eddie Capparucci, has learned that self-destructive behaviors correlate with the emotional pain and trauma that haunts the Inner Child. Rather than developing strategies and techniques to manage your behavior, you are invited to something better: to connect with and strengthen the child within you."

—Jay Stringer, Psychotherapist, and author of Unwanted: How Sexual Brokenness Reveals Our Way to Healing

"Too often, when dealing with sexual addictions in men, we remain focused on the symptoms of the behaviors rather than peeling back these external layers to uncover the wounded Inner Child. Eddie Capparucci has done a masterful job of exposing the key emotional triggers that lie at the root of most men's sexual addictions. With grace and clarity, Going Deeper will help men understand and respond to these triggers in practical, redemptive ways. I highly recommend this book to both the men who struggle with sexually addictive strongholds and the people who love and care for them."

—Jonathan Daugherty, Founder-President Bebroken Ministries

"Eddie Capparucci has hit the nail on the head with this book. He goes directly to the core issues of why people seek comfort from sex addictions and pornography. By describing the 12 reasons why men abuse sex, he stresses the importance of healing the Inner Child, whose legitimate, unmet needs to create chaos and addiction in adult life. This is a valuable and practical read on an issue that has reached epidemic proportions with the advent of the internet."

—*Esly Regina Carvalho, Ph.D., author of Healing the Folks Who Live Inside.*

"Eddie has done a wonderful job in identifying the core issues that negatively impact a sex addict's life in a simple and understandable way. We all carry our training (experiences) from childhood, and we must identify and understand them to create the "New Man." Men struggling with sexual addiction who read this book will not only start the journey to uncover their Inner Child but will also find practical skills to move toward overall health."

—*Troy Snyder, LPC, CCSAS, CPCS, Christian Sex Addiction Specialists International Board Member*

"Eddie Capparucci is a steady guide in the rocky terrain of navigating sexual addiction and examining the foundations of its origins. What a fabulous resource for folks to begin to look deeply at how their story shapes their sexuality. Thank you, Eddie, for providing this map and showing us the way toward liberation."

—*Andrew J. Bauman, author of The Psychology of Porn*

"This book is a must-read for men working on long-term change and freedom from sexual addiction. Eddie has it right: acknowledging and comforting our Inner Child while setting loving limits around his behavior is the key to enduring recovery."

—Troy Haas, MDiv, CADC II, CSAT, CEO & Co-Founder HopeQuest Ministry Group

"Getting to the root of problematic sexual behavior and healing wounds is key to recovery and transformation. Eddie connects with the reader with great tools and resources for healing the child within. This isn't just another "Inner Child" book. It's a tool that can be transformative in your journey."

—Richard Blankenship, NCC, CPCS, CBTS, CSRRS, Clinical Director of Capstone Center for Sexual Recovery & Transformation

"This valuable addition to the field explains in plain language how early life experiences can influence present-day behavior, especially for people who struggle with sexual behavior that goes against their commitments and values. The "plain talking" style is amazingly effective in talking about a topic that can be difficult for some to understand. The ability to identify the needs of the wounded Inner Child is essential for a person who is wrestling with impulses and fantasies that may at first seem confusing. This book helps the reader ask the right questions. It is a practical book that will help many people."

—Bill Herring, LCSW, CSAT

THE ESSENCE OF CHANGE

"This is the verdict: Light has come into the world, but people loved darkness instead of light because their deeds were evil. Everyone who does evil hates the light and will not come into the light for fear that their deeds will be exposed. But whoever lives by the truth comes into the light so that it may be seen plainly that what they have done has been done in the sight of God." —John 3: 19-21

"I hope this book will take you on a journey that leads you out of the darkness and into the light."

– Eddie Capparucci, Ph.D., LPC, C-CSAS

TABLE OF CONTENTS

FOREWORD

When Eddie asked me to write the foreword to this book, I must admit my "Inner Child" was triggered, and I freaked out a bit. Even some of my old shameful lies of perfectionism leaped to the surface, trying to point out this would be just another opportunity for me to fail or disappoint.

But thankfully, because of precisely the kind of work Eddie has outlined in this book, I can say I knew how to respond to the little, scared boy inside me. After years of personal investment in this kind of work, I know my true self; I value and respect who my Inner Child is and how God's grace has embraced him in all his brokenness to help him "grow up" and enjoy life.

Maybe you picked up this book because what you have been doing to overcome your destructive behaviors has not been working. You know something is missing. You want answers to more in-depth questions that your current methods of help have not been addressing.

Good news! That is what Going Deeper is all about. Helping you understand and respond to your patterns of brokenness with grace and truth.

WHAT IS THE REAL PROBLEM?

Often, when people reach out for help with sexual struggles and strongholds, they focus primarily on their symptoms. Their behaviors are readily seen, and the effects of such actions leave a trail of wounded and weary loved ones. But only focusing on redirecting or eliminating unhealthy behaviors misses the mark of what needs to be addressed: the inner person. More specifically, the Inner Child.

Did you know the decisions you make daily are not random or arbitrary? The way you make choices (good and bad) has a pattern that is stable and repeatable. But often, we do not pay much attention to the underlying thoughts, feelings, or historical events that shaped these patterns. We feel frustrated, ashamed, or angry about our unhealthy sexual behaviors. We feel stuck.

What if you could know what is driving your unhealthy choices? What if you could get to the root of the problem? What if you could understand yourself and your patterns in a way that brings about real change in your life? What if?

Such knowledge will not come by "trying harder" to behave because behavior is not where the real problem lies. You and I need our hearts to be changed. We need our Inner Child to be called out and embraced and transformed by the grace and truth of God and His Word.

If you do not address your brokenness at its deepest level, you likely will not experience the most profound healing. Therefore, dive deep into this book's pages if you want more than just a behavior management system, more than a list of never-ending rigid rules that have left you hopeless. Open yourself up to the possibilities that God has a hope and future for you that is brimming with peace and joy even during your brokenness as you travel the road of healing your Inner Child.

A Word of Warning

Before you turn the page and start working on your heart, I must offer a warning. Digging deep into your history and hurts is not light or easy. Taking an honest look at your Inner Child in all his or her brokenness can be a taxing venture emotionally, spiritually, mentally, and even physically.

Please do not travel this road alone. Invite some trusted friends to do this work with you. Invest in counseling. Connect with pastors and peers in your church. Such a community will provide you the courage to do hard things and deepen the vital relationships to the abundant life Jesus wants you to experience. It is a win-win.

Grace Abounds

One final note of encouragement as you read this material: God's grace abounds! You will likely have many similar experiences to what I mentioned at the beginning of this foreword. Your Inner Child will be exposed and triggered, causing all kinds of reactions that may feel unpleasant or even scary. Shame may wash over you. Fear may surround you. Your past sins will leap in front of your face. Guilt will try to drag you away. This is normal – and God is not deterred by it. Let me paint a picture of how your heavenly Father sees you, even in all your brokenness.

His eyes are fixed on you, never blinking. His arms are around you, never letting go.

His mind is filled with good thoughts toward you, never ashamed. His voice is singing over you with songs of deliverance, never condemning.

His Spirit is in you, never leaving.

You are loved, and nothing can change that.

May you experience the abundance of God's grace as you go deeper with your Inner Child.

Jonathan Daugherty

Founder, President

BeBroken Ministries

INTRODUCTION

UNDERSTANDING THE KID RUNS THE SHOW

I bet you are exhausted. And I would not be surprised if you feel hopeless. I know I was. Trying to manage our Problematic Sexual Behaviors (PSBs) can leave us feeling frustrated and shameful. We read countless books, articles, and blogs, attend support groups and intensive weekends, install, and activate device monitoring software, meet with accountability partners, and journal until our hands are cramped. But here we are, still knee-deep in the cesspool. And we keep asking, "Why can't I get it right?"

The answer to that frustrating question is we have not been examining the true nature of our problem. Because if we did, we would find the road to recovery from PSBs goes through our childhood.

Based on my work with hundreds of men who have struggled with sexual integrity issues, I have learned that PSBs directly correlate to the emotional pain and trauma that haunts the Inner Child. By learning how to connect, comfort, and soothe the Child, we can experience successful outcomes in managing our PSBs. (Please note, throughout this book, I use the term PSBs, which covers porn and sex addiction.)

In my clinical practice, the men I work with represent all racial and social demographics and engage in various occupations ranging from judges and clergy to teachers and assembly-line workers. My clients also have included National Football League and Major League Baseball players and television personalities. This disorder does not discriminate.

I should pause here to explain that this book is written from the perspective of men who struggle with PSBs. I am fully aware women also deal with PSBs. It is so critical that I have teamed up with two female clinicians to write *Going Deeper for Women: How the Inner Child Impacts Love and Porn Addiction*.

Pornography viewing is growing at a rapid rate among younger females. So, while this book's content focuses on men, the concepts of this recovery approach are also beneficial for women.

As you will learn in reading this book, I believe the most critical objective in this process is pursuing and achieving personal insight.

And when it comes to obtaining insight – the **why** question is the key. *"Why do you think, feel, and act as you do?"* And in this case, *"Why does sex have a stronghold on you?"*

After years of helping men focus on self-reflection, I have realized that knowing why we do what we do dramatically increases our ability to shift away from undesirable behaviors. Knowing why you elect to engage in certain destructive activities will empower you to make choices that lead to healthy behaviors. But knowing why requires you to engage with your Inner Child because it is within him the in-depth answers to your struggles await.

PSBs are not about sex. They result from a man's inability to deal with his anxiety and manage emotional pain and distress without distracting himself with sexual activities. Now, that is not a new finding. Many clinicians have discussed the core issue that impacts PSBs. However, few have explained in-depth and identified many of the core emotional wounds men harbor. That is where this book is unique.

In my clinical practice, I realized the most effective resource for identifying and managing core emotions that trigger addictive behavior is for men to connect with and understand their Inner Child.

It is worth saying again, "The road to recovery from sexual addiction goes through your childhood."

As you will learn, your Inner Child is trapped in a distressing time warp where various traumas and neglect occurred. Unfortunately, his method of decision-making is grounded entirely in emotional thinking skills. Therefore, he is the storage unit containing deeply rooted emotional pain that has been pushed and cast aside. It is a storage unit you have not entered in years or decades and contains hurtful memories suffered as a child and teenager. Your Inner Child uses the storage unit to keep locked away hurtful words and actions that left deeply repressed scars.

However, just because negative memories are repressed does not mean you have escaped them. And this is where your Inner Child enters the picture. As he witnesses current negative events in your life today, he often incorrectly correlates them to past painful memories he feels are like what you are experiencing.

While you are unaware of the negative memories your Inner Child is focusing on, you realize your anxiety is heightening. You contribute it to the negative event that recently occurred. But what is really happening is your Inner Child has subconsciously raised your level of anxiousness, and he will soon drive you to escape your emotional discomfort by engaging in destructive sexual behaviors. He is running the show.

As one of my clients said, "The main problem is I don't even feel like I'm the one making a choice. I seem to gravitate toward reckless behaviors. It's like I'm on autopilot."

Just like my client, it is time to take control of your PSBs. No more autopilot. It is time for you to take charge by learning how to manage your Child. I want to empower you. I want you to start running the show.

You are about to discover a new road to managing PSBs based on years of successful outcomes in clinical settings across the globe. And that road to healing goes right through your childhood. Hang on; this is a ride that can change your life forever.

In this second edition of Going Deeper, we introduce three new Inner Children to the family – the Unwanted, Spiritually Wounded, and Enmeshed children. The updated book also offers more resources and updated graphics.

You can find more about the Inner Child and PSBs, including an online recovery program, at www.innerchild-sexaddiction.com

Eddie Capparucci, Ph.D., LPC, C-CSAS

Editing Note: You will find the word 'child' capitalized in certain places, not others. When capitalized, the word refers to a Child in my model. All other references to the word 'child' are lowercase.

CHAPTER 1

It is Nurture, Not Nature

"Clocks will go as they are set, but man, irregular man, is never constant, never certain."

—Thomas Otway

Let me start with a simple confession.

I struggled with Problematic Sexual Behaviors (PSBs), which, in my early years, caused tremendous havoc to myself and others. I am broken based on many factors that occurred in my childhood that resulted in the development of an attachment disorder, anxiety, an addictive brain, and a compulsive disorder. None of these are excuses for my behaviors but simply rationales to explain why I did what I did. I alone am responsible for my destructive actions. I own my insensitive and callous actions. I am also fortunate to have been in recovery for over 25 years and continue to thrive.

Accepting we are sexually broken leaves us feeling like warped, twisted perverts. It makes us feel dirty. And the thought of someone discovering our dark secret makes us want to vomit in shame.

Our undesired sexual behaviors haunt most of us who have been trapped in the vicious cycle of abusing sex while agonizing over why we cannot stop. After years of failing to end our addictive behaviors, we believe there is not much we can do about the endless stream of sexual thoughts and images that litter our minds throughout the day.

In fact, for as long as we can remember, sex has been the focal point of our lives. We waste hours trying to find it. And once we have it, we cannot stop indulging. There never seems to be enough, and worst yet, there is no shut-off valve. What we love the most, we hate the most. Being trapped in our PSBs is like residing in Hell.

If not for the insanity of the PSBs, the idea of sexual images continuously floating through our heads or engaging in endless sexual activities would almost seem natural. Why? Because lust is a natural response for men. Part of the reason is men are easily visually stimulated.

MANAGING LUST IS NOT A PROBLEM FOR EVERY MAN

It does not take much to draw lust in most men. Sights such as a woman's bare neck exposed when her hair is pulled up to the ankle strap of a woman's shoe can be thrilling for a man, depending on what triggers his lust. Sexual desire is simply part of a man's DNA. But it is essential to understand this lust can be effectively managed when men understand what leads to their insatiable hunger.

Most men learn to control their lust and do not engage sexually in a way that objectifies, demeans, dishonors, or degrades women. So, what makes these men different from those who battle with sexual integrity? There are several factors.

- They were taught to identify, process, and express their emotions, including hurtful and painful feelings
- They witnessed a healthy and ideal model of intimacy displayed by parents that they could replicate
- They learned to respect women and admire their beauty instead of objectifying their body parts
- They were not subjected to or had limited emotional, mental, physical, or sexual traumas
- They were not neglected
- They do not experience elevated levels of anxiety

Can you pick up a similarity in the six reasons above? Each of the rationales represents an environment in which a child receives healthy instruction and guidance while at the same time not being subjected to trauma/neglect that leads to elevated levels of anxiety. For the most part – unlike their counterparts – these men grew up with little need to distract themselves from emotional torment as children or teenagers. Instead, there was an adult they could rely upon to help them process their emotional pain and deal with it in a healthy manner.

While escaping emotional distress is central to all addictions, the issue with PSBs is that most men do not realize they abuse sex to avoid emotional discomfort. Instead, they see themselves as:

- Highly sexual individuals
- Perverted
- Defective
- Lacking the social skills needed to be involved in "real" relationships

Also, men who struggle with PSBs do not engage in sex as God designed it. The healthy purpose of sex beyond procreation is to enhance emotional intimacy in a relationship. Instead, they use sex as a self-soothing coping mechanism that produces an adrenaline rush powerful enough to block out the most troubling emotional pain.

However, these rationales do not explain the actual reason(s) why men engage in undesired sexual behaviors. These guys have done an excellent job of repressing emotional pain for years. In fact, they struggle to identify any emotions except for anger, sadness, happiness, loneliness, and fear. This means they do not understand **why** they are abusing sex as a means of escape. To them, it has merely become a bad habit.

As a counselor certified in treating PSBs and more than 25 years in recovery, I often hear from men when I start working with them: "*I don't understand why I act this way.*"

This book aims to provide insight to help you and your spouse understand **why** you turn to sex as an escape mechanism from emotional misery. But more importantly, I will show you a proven approach to sitting with your emotional pain points while managing your addictive behaviors effectively.

So why is **why** so important? I am glad you asked. And the best way to explain it is to share a story regarding one of my clients. (BTW, the case studies in this book are real; however, names and some of the details have been changed to maintain clients' anonymity.)

BRAD'S STORY

Brad had it all. A wife who was a former beauty queen. Two healthy and bright children about to enter middle school. A well-paying job that saw him accelerate up the senior management ranks. He was an elder in his church and respected by co-workers, friends, and neighbors. To everyone on the outside looking in, Brad had it all together. But it was the furthest thing from the truth.

> ## MOST MEN DO NOT REALIZE THEY ABUSE SEX TO AVOID EMOTIONAL DISCOMFORT

Brad suffered from full-blown PSBs involving pornography, affairs, and liaisons with escorts. What started as sneaking peeks at his older brother's Penthouse magazines continued to manifest over the years, escalating in intensity and frequency. Early in their marriage, Brad's wife discovered he viewed porn but elected not to acknowledge it but instead justified it as something all men did. Fourteen years later, she caught Brad sleeping with a neighbor's wife.

When they came to see me for counseling, Brad's wife, Tami, kept repeating, *"I don't understand. Why would you do this to us?"* She could not comprehend how a man who seemed to have the world in his hands would risk everything for reckless, physical thrills.

And as she kept turning to Brad, seeking a reason he acted so irresponsibly, he had no real answer for her. *"It seems like a natural reaction,"* he said, responding to her, ignoring the box of tissues, and using his shirt sleeve to wipe away his own tears. *"I could be working at my computer, and I switch to a porn site. Or I could finish a business call and automatically dial the number of one of the women I have been carrying on with. There's no rhyme or reason for what I do. I just do it. I guess I am a pervert."*

"That's the first thing you said in days, I believe," said Tami, turning away from him in disgust, sobbing as she buried her head in her hands.

Knowing "Why" is a Key

Being unable to understand why we abuse sex is the number one frustration for men and their partners when a sexual integrity issue is first exposed. The inability to reconcile the why question leaves everyone involved feeling helpless and hopeless.

"I have been dealing with his selfish bull for years," shouted Amanda, sitting on the edge of the couch to ensure I could feel her exasperation in trying to cope with her husband, Todd. *"I catch him watching porn, and he promises to stop. And what happens? A couple of months later, I caught him*

again. I can't tell you how long this has been going on, but I do know I can't take it much longer. It's obvious he'd rather look at a computer screen and jerk off than have sex with me."

Those words from Amanda's lips were piercing, and I could see Todd deflated as shame swept over him. His wife cannot understand how the man who once desired her physically prefers to be stimulated by sexual imagery. She finds it insulting and demeaning. And she is right to feel so. It trashes her self-worth and leaves her feeling less like a woman. His behavior is childish and hurtful.

That is why men in recovery must be challenged to understand the depth of their partners' emotional anguish resulting from the betrayal. As I tell my clients, you have three jobs. The first is making your recovery a priority, the second is actively participating in your wife's healing by taking consistent actions to make her feel safe, and the third is learning to become emotionally developed. Through my work, I estimate nine out of 10 men who struggle with PSBs are emotionally undeveloped.

You can learn more about the lack of emotional development and its negative impact on relationships in my book, *Why Men Struggle to Love: Overcoming Relational Blind Spots*. It helps answer the question, *"is being sober enough?"*

A CHARACTER FLAW

Hurting Amanda was never Todd's intent. He is still very much attracted to his wife and would welcome the opportunity to be sexually intimate with her, but she has refused since discovering his pornography practices. She feels deceived and cannot imagine giving herself to him for fear he would fantasize instead of being mindful of her. In her eyes, Todd is not emotionally safe. Unfortunately, she is right.

PSBs create a vicious and destructive cycle that keeps couples feeling defeated and disappointed. But it is a cycle that can be broken when we have valuable insight that answers a critical question. And that question is **why**.

For years, I have asked new clients why they abuse sex. Here is what I have heard them say.

- "I have no idea."
- "I wish I knew."
- "I think it's just who I am."
- "It is the way God made me."
- "I think I am simply perverted."
- "I'm sick."
- "I'm disgusting."
- "I'm a loser."
- "I'm a bad man."
- "I'm mentally disturbed."
- "I am too self-absorbed."
- "I am stupid."
- "I have no willpower."

In treating men struggling with PSBs, I have heard those comments and more. But I will let you in on a secret. Those answers above are all incorrect. Without a clear-cut rationale for why we do what we do, we will default to believing we suffer from a character flaw or physiological disorder. In our minds, our obsessed focus on sex results from a perverted mind or an overactive sexual libido.

GOING DEEPER TO UNDERSTAND "WHY" PLAYS AN ESSENTIAL ROLE IN HELPING MANAGE YOUR PSBS

What about you? What is your answer to the **why** question? Is your response as harsh as some of the labels listed?

I am convinced I am hard-wired differently than other guys," said Connor, explaining his habit of spending nearly $250 weekly on live sex webcasts. "There is no other explanation for why I am consumed with sexual thoughts around the clock. I can't get them out of my head."

Connor is right; he is hard-wired to abuse sex, but not due to anything biological or physiological. Connor's obsession with sex was developed to serve as a defense mechanism to distract from emotional pain and its resulting anxiety caused by people and events at a younger age. Connor learned to block out emotional anguish by engaging in distracting activities that stimulated or numbed him to protect himself. And at some point, his go-to distraction became sex.

To straighten out his wiring, Connor will need to uncover the true root of his PSBs and the core emotional triggers that activate them. He will need to go deeper to answer why.

"If you want to understand why you are addicted to something, you have to understand the conditions that keep

9

your addiction in place," writes Jay Stringer, a counselor, ordained minister, and author of the book Unwanted. "The choice of unwanted sexual behavior is never accidental. There is always a reason. Your path to freedom from destructive sexual behavior begins with finding the unique reasons behind yours."

Well said.

HER NEED FOR EMPATHY

As you read this book, you will understand that discovering the origin of PSBs is vital in the recovery process. The key to unlocking the power of PSBs is to uncover why they manifested in the first place. Answers to the *"why I abused sex"* question provide relief and hope we can finally manage our PSBs. And this is the alternative to shame and frustration.

Guess what? Your spouse needs to know the answer to the **why** question too! Knowing why you engage in reckless behavior assists her in understanding your PSBs are not about sex. This insight helps to clear up the misconception she is dealing with "an out-of-control pervert" who will never stop acting out. The answer to why provides both of you a sense of hope needed to manage the behaviors and build a new relationship together.

When a wife or partner understands why, it opens the door for them to develop empathy, which is needed for a couple to reconnect. This powerful emotion allows those betrayed to see the addict through a softer pair of eyes that are not as condemning and judgmental.

"I was shocked to learn what Matt had been doing had nothing to do with sex or me," said Rachel, whose husband had spent thousands of dollars at massage parlors. "It was quite a relief to understand there was some rationale for the insane things he was involved in."

Now, do not take Rachel's comments wrong. She is not condoning Matt's PSBs; she could not comprehend how he had acted out in such a destructive manner. *"Just because I now understand doesn't mean I am ready to forgive,"* she continued, ensuring I knew where she stood in her recovery process. *"But I could see the day coming. Before this, I had no hope of ever forgiving him. It is obvious he's been dealing with a lot from his childhood that I never knew. And it spilled over into our marriage."*

When a woman develops empathy for her troubled partner, she indicates an understanding of his problem. However, she is not saying she accepts the behavior in any way, shape, or form. She continues to despise it. But by becoming empathetic, a woman can find ways to heal and ultimately embrace her partner once again if – and this is a BIG if – she sees he is committed to transforming.

She is saying, "I understand why you did what you did. It all makes sense to me. However, it still hurts me, so what are you doing to fix your problem?"

Understanding the rationale for his compulsive acts does not give a man a free pass. He cannot use these insights as excuses and expect everyone to sympathize with him. Instead, he must take full responsibility for the pain he has caused others.

"It's a relief to understand the reasons behind my addiction," said Billy, who ran through two marriages due to his expensive escort habit. "But that does not change the fact I have messed up and hurt people, especially my ex-wives. That's on me. I own that."

Men like Billy must show a commitment to recovery while demonstrating the desire to transform and change their hearts. The men who "own" their actions are ultimately the men who will succeed in this battle. These men show:

- Deep understanding of the harm they have caused
- True sense of remorse
- Hunger for insight into the origins of their compulsive behaviors
- Passion and pursuit of recovery
- Willingness to participate in a community with other men who struggle
- Desire to deepen the emotional bond with their spouse, family, and God by strengthening their emotional skills
- Commitment to develop a servant's heart and put the needs and desires of others before himself

SEEKING SEXUAL INTEGRITY

By asking the why question, we begin a journey in which we are not merely attempting to change our insensitive and damaging behaviors but, more importantly, to embrace and achieve integrity. Our focus will center on consistent, personal self-reflection and aims to understand better the rationale for our thoughts, emotions, and behaviors. It launches us on a mission to change our hearts, which goes far beyond merely correcting our behaviors. We are genuinely becoming men of sexual integrity.

What is sexual integrity? It has less to do with sex and more with a man's character. Sexual integrity is our commitment to transparency and honesty about our sexual desires and actions. It also involves honoring and respecting others and ourselves when it comes to sex.

> "I urge you, brothers and sisters, in view of God's mercy, to offer your bodies as a living sacrifice, holy and pleasing to God—this is your true and proper worship" Rom. 12:1 NIV

Sexual integrity involves sacrifice, which means we cannot carelessly engage in any sexual pleasures we desire. While there is no doubt sex provides great physical, mental, and emotional satisfaction, in being men of integrity, we learn to check our lust at the door and live as Spiritual beings, devoted to honoring God, others, and ourselves.

IS PORN REALLY A PROBLEM?

A significant hurdle I often experience with men who view pornography is they see nothing wrong with their actions. They think pornography is acceptable. Some even think it is healthy. No man can escape from PSBs until they first learn to hate their actions and understand they are unacceptable. Nothing is honorable about pornography, which teaches men to objectify while dehumanizing and degrading women and other men.

I ask men who think porn is harmless the following question. "Tell me the time you asked a 12-year-old girl what she wanted to be when she grew up, and her answer was, 'I want to take off my clothes and have sex in front of a camera with strange men and women.'"

I have yet to have a man answer that question. Do I believe some of these young girls exist? Sadly, yes, I do. But I guarantee they have undergone severe trauma that has crushed and eroded their self-worth. Someone or multiple people have hurt them very badly.

Pornography is also a health hazard because it is a steppingstone for escalating reckless and risky sexual behavior. Far too many men have found themselves moving to other destructive sexual practices as the stimulation generated by pornography starts to fade.

"I never thought I would ever visit prostitutes, but I wanted so desperately to engage in sexual acts I saw in porn," said Klaus, who is still struggling to deal with his wife's decision to divorce after discovering his behavior. "For years, I thought pornography was all I needed to satisfy my lust. But it reached a point where I wanted to experience what I had been viewing. If I had given up porn earlier, I would not be in the mess I am today."

For this journey, our focus is on building a new legacy. And that cannot be achieved by merely applying behavioral techniques to managing our PSBs. There is no doubt technologies such as accountability and filtering software – such as Covenant Eyes – and limiting access to the Internet and finances are valuable in helping manage PSBs during the early stages of treatment.

But once again, they are focused more on behavioral changes instead of generating integrity and transforming men's hearts. These tools are much needed stop gaps that we use when helping to re-boot the addictive brain. A reboot, which takes hold at approximately 90 days, eliminates sexual stimuli, allowing the brain to quiet down and begin to return to its natural neurological state. However, it may take several years for this process to be completed.

MEN WHO ENDURED TRAUMAS, AS WELL AS NEGLECT, ARE MORE AT RISK OF ENGAGING IN PROBLEMATIC SEXUAL BEHAVIORS

I get a little concerned when a wife comes into counseling with her husband for their initial session and proudly has him display the flip phone, she had required him to buy to replace his smartphone. She seems to believe cutting off his access to porn is the end-all of the problem. Wrong.

CHANGING YOUR HEART

I agree with using devices that limit exposure to sexual images, inappropriate apps, and chatting for a period as a man learns to manage his PSBs. How long? That depends upon the individual and his dedication to the recovery process. Some men may need longer behavioral modification practices than others.

However, I also know behavior modification is nothing more than a band-aid if we do not get to the root of PSBs. We may prevent him from acting out because he does not have access, but that solution does not teach him how to become a man of integrity.

These restrictions do not teach how to deal with temptations and ultimately manage the disorder. Instead, a betrayed spouse attempts to control the situation by tying the betrayer's hands and locking him in a box. It does little to change the heart. Worst yet, he may decide to escape from the box one day, and the results will be ugly.

I worked with a client who had a porn addiction. To ease her anxiety, his wife removed his access to television, radio, and the Internet. He had a flip phone and was required to check in with her every hour when away from home. He was cut off from his friends. The only books he could read were recovery and Christian-focused. She had placed him in a deep box. I should mention he had been sober from porn for three years before coming to see me.

After working with them for a short time, I discharged them, recommending she seek help for her past trauma that I believed was exacerbating her current trauma. For five years after being discharged, he called me on the day of his anniversary to acknowledge another year of sobriety while noting the relationship had not improved. Then, one year, I did not receive a call from him and have not since. My fear is he broke out of his box.

THE NEVER-ENDING MADNESS

I have worked with men who have been through counseling for PSBs multiple times and attended workshops, seminars, and intensives, and nothing stuck. The behavior modification techniques they were provided proved short-lived, and their initial hope of *"getting it right this time"* was lost with their first relapse. If you read NoFap discussion boards, you will notice most comments focus on relapse. It breaks my heart to see all of those men struggling.

The behavioral approaches soon lose their impact by never exploring the why question regarding their PSBs. Again, there is a place for behavior modification in managing PSBs. I use them in my practice. But we must go deeper into the treatment process.

On-and-off recovery is a painful cycle leading to despair and hopelessness not only for the men caught in the addictive cycle but also for the women who love them.

"It never seems to end," said Karen as she sat with a box of tissues in her lap and a discarded pile of wet tissues at her feet. "How many chances do I need to give him? I am at the end of my rope and don't know how much more I have left."

Karen described her relationship with her husband, Barry, a porn junkie since 13. Now approaching 34 and married for 10 years, Barry struggles with pornography despite working with four different counselors, reading numerous books, having several accountability partners, working a 12-step program, attending a recovery retreat weekend, and being on medication.

But when Barry was asked to discuss why he had PSBs, he was at a loss for words. *"I never thought about it,"* he said, standing and staring out the window in my office. *"And no counselor has asked me the question before. I would certainly like to know because it breaks my heart that Karen still believes it has something to do with her."*

It is unfortunate, but the story of Barry and Karen is familiar. Years after PSBs had been exposed, many couples still struggled to reconnect because of their fears and wounds. They live with pessimism and feel helpless to re-engage because they are surrounded by daily tension and worry about the unknown. She cannot move toward him, fearing more betrayals, while he fears being unable to manage the PSBs. It is a lose-lose situation that could be improved if they took the first step and understood the answer to the **why** question.

But understand this: knowing why your PSBs manifested is NOT the only insight and strategic tool you need to manage the disorder. However, in my mind, it is the driving force that will empower you on this recovery journey. This new sense of empowerment will help you implement the tools necessary to manage your PSBs.

"While healing does not occur by knowing exactly how and why the addiction developed, it does come when the addict learns to put these experiences into perspective by acknowledging how these experiences have had an impact," writes Dr. Kevin B. Skinner in his book entitled Treating Pornography Addiction: The Essential Tools for Recovery.

"Then, with this knowledge, he will know how to do things differently in the future."

Dr. Skinner points out the importance of understanding why and how these answers can change our decision-making process. Whenever we act out, it correlates to a core emotional trigger. Remember those three words – core emotional triggers –are critical in this process, and we will refer to them repeatedly throughout this book. Our core emotional triggers are far more powerful than visual or environmental triggers. That is not to say these triggers are not impactful – they are. But core emotional triggers activate your Inner Child, which is when chaos enters the picture.

NEED TO IDENTIFY CORE EMOTIONAL TRIGGERS

But often, we fail to notice core emotional triggers when they occur. Why? Because we do not know what core emotional triggers will activate our acting out! By not identifying and understanding the reason(s) why we abuse sex, we are limiting our ability to manage destructive behaviors. You do not know what you do not know.

Without vital information, it is difficult to solve any problem we face. For example, doctors cannot heal a patient until they have a diagnosis. And that is what we are talking about here – embarking on a journey to diagnose the cause of our PSBs, which starts with answering the **why** question. The answer to why will lead us to uncover our core emotional triggers and freedom from PSBs.

I believe addicts are not born; they are created. I developed this opinion through my work with men struggling with PSBs and in counseling at a residential program treating men and women dealing with alcohol and drug addictions. Over the years, I have come to believe people who endure trauma/neglect at an early age – including physical, emotional, mental, or sexual abuse – are more at risk of succumbing to addictions.

I also have learned that men struggle to deal with difficult emotions because they are fear-based. As men, the last thing we want to admit is we are fearful. But the truth is many men are afraid of feeling. I have also uncovered another vital factor that serves as the primary driver of all addictions.

The Inner Child.

CHAPTER 2

Understanding Your Inner Child

"The child is in me still and sometimes not so still."

—Mr. Rogers

As you dig deeper into this book, you probably ask yourself, "Who is the Inner Child, and how could he possibly have anything to do with my addiction?"

Frankly, I do not blame you for thinking such a thought. The concept of the Inner Child is nothing new. However, it has never been applied to helping men manage their struggles with sex and porn. So, let us briefly examine who this Child is and why it would benefit you to know him better.

UNTAPPING THE WOUNDS OF YOUR INNER CHILD BRINGS YOU PEACE

Our Inner Child is representative of our subconscious emotional and mental pain. He is derived from people and events in our lives that resulted in trauma and/or neglect.

The Inner Child, who has experienced frightening and confusing moments throughout your young life, sits in the background of your subconscious. And while he may produce a constant, low-level grumbling of anxiety in some of us, his actual presence is felt when he becomes activated by core emotional triggers. See, I told you to remember those three words.

The concept of the Inner Child is nothing new. Many philosophers and mental healthcare professionals have discussed and debated it for centuries, and many aspects of the Inner Child have been reviewed and written. However, utilizing the Inner Child to treat PSBs is a unique and exciting approach that has not been done in the past.

By the way, an excellent book regarding the Inner Child is entitled *Healing the Child Within* by Charles Whitman, which examines many dimensions of the Child, including his playfulness. However, this book will focus on a single component of the Inner Child – his emotional pain. Why? Because children's unresolved emotional pain points lead men to engage in destructive sexual behaviors.

TWO WORLDS COLLIDE

But how can unresolved pain from our past lead you to act out? Easy. Your Inner Child correlates adverse events and circumstances you face daily with painful memories of past events that seem remarkably similar to him. To make matters worse, in many cases, his interpretation of current circumstances does not match up with the painful events of the past. But it seems that way to him, which gets us in trouble.

INTRODUCING THE INNER CHILD ACTIVATION PROCESS

Negative Event Occurs → Releases Core Emotional Trigger → Activates Inner Child ↓ Recalls Past Pain Point ← Discomfort Level Increases ← Seek Escape Through Destructive Behaviors

As this process unfolds, your anxiety steadily increases. You think it is due to the current event, but it is more than that. Your Inner Child is subconsciously bringing past emotional pain to the surface, exacerbating the situation, and heightening your anxiety.

Since those with addictive brains – such as yourself – cannot sit with emotional pain, they learn at a young age to distract themselves with behaviors that stimulate or numb. Over time, these behaviors can become addictive.

For example, your wife asks you to stop by the store to pick up milk, but you left your brain at your desk at work and forgot your assignment. When she asks, *"Where's the milk?"* your brain returns, and you realize, *"Oops."* Before you can even apologize, she yells and says how selfish and inconsiderate you are. You try to defend yourself, but her sharp sword is no match for the white handkerchief you are waving. And while the yelling is terrible enough, she takes action that activates your Inner Child. She walks out of the house, heading to the store.

While this leaves you annoyed at yourself for not paying more attention to your chore list, it has your Inner Child screaming.

Why? Because when you were a child, your mother, when angry, would punish you by exiting the room, leaving you feeling abandoned. It was a tactic she knew would leave you wondering if she would never return (it is called emotional manipulation). The "milk" event has left your Inner Child correlating your wife's current behavior to your mom's previous behavior. Two worlds have collided – the present and the past. And with this, your risk of acting out has increased.

I will share more about the connection between past and current circumstances when we get to the Inner Child Activation Process Chart later in this chapter.

THE CHILD IS A RUNNER

It is essential to understand our Inner Child, while very fearful, is also extremely powerful. He has taught you to use the coping mechanisms of distraction and withdrawal to escape from dealing with painful emotions. And in many cases, he goes a step further to protect himself by putting up walls that assist in concealing these complex and hurtful emotions. Your Inner Child is a runner. He runs and hides to pretend the emotional pain does not exist.

The problem is when he runs, he takes you along with him. You have learned to be a runner, seeking an escape (your addictive behaviors) to distract yourself from what you should be doing – processing emotional pain points that are part of your life.

Knowing your Inner Child is locked in a time warp is essential. He is forever at ground zero, reliving various painful events you suffered as a child, young boy, and teen. The Child is surrounded by scarring memories such as:

- Dad referring to you as a little girl
- Dealing with neighborhood bullies
- A slap across the face by your mom
- Freezing in front of the class when giving an oral presentation and hearing the laughter and taunts
- Being the only one among your friends not to make the Little League team
- Watching Dad shove Mom during another night of fighting
- Your brother sexually abusing you
- Being told you are stupid

Unfortunately, the list goes on and on.

TAKE A MOMENT: What humiliating or hurtful moments can you recall suffering as a child or adolescent? This topic is difficult but integral to understanding and connecting with your Inner Child. Do not be surprised as you start to write that you recall memories long forgotten. It is ok. You are starting to obtain valuable insights to help manage your PSBs. As you get going, you will need a journal to capture the information you uncover.

During our journey, you will discover your Inner Child comes across as exceptionally selfish – but not because of his own doing. No adult was available to teach him how to process complex and troubling circumstances and feelings. So, therefore he turned inward to protect himself. His worldview became, *"I have to deal with my scary feelings alone."*

As children, if we do not receive guidance and direction on recognizing and managing our emotions, we will have trouble regulating our emotional temperaments. That is a central issue with our Inner Child; he is super sensitive and easily triggered by negative events. When the Child gets started (basically, he is having a tantrum because he is fearful of the emotional pain he is experiencing), it leads to bad decision-making if you are not mindful of what is occurring.

Oh, I forgot! Men who deal with PSBs are not mindful. Can you see the potential dilemma?

Our Inner Child does not think about others' feelings or the consequences of his actions. He only wants the pain to go away. That is why when a wife asks, *"What leads you to turn to pornography so often when you have me available,"* she often gets the answer, *"I don't know."* Your Inner Child is not concerned with your wife's or anyone's feelings, for that matter.

WHAT THE INNER CHILD WANTS

There is only one goal our Inner Child has – to seek comfort. He is locked in survival mode and will do anything not to experience the troubling emotions he endured in the past. To avoid " feeling," the Child has learned to use often destructive behaviors to distract and self-soothe. Unfortunately for you and me, he discovered sex as the ultimate source of comfort. In seeking ways to avoid sitting with painful emotions, he learned sex provides an adrenaline rush unlike anything he has ever experienced. It is even more exciting than Disneyland.

THE ADRENALINE RUSH PROVIDED BY SEXUAL BEHAVIORS CAN HELP MASK ANY EMOTIONAL DISTRESS

"You can never believe how satisfying watching pornography was for me as a young teenager," recalls Joe, who watched his parents go through a messy divorce when he was 12. "All my pain and anger toward my parents evaporated the moment the first image appeared. Like magic, porn washed away all my pain. And once you learn how to escape, it's hard not to go back to it. You end up using it to remove all discomfort."

"I equate it to anesthesia," said Ted, who first saw pornography at the tender age of nine. "It blocks out everything troubling in your life. In fact, it serves as a cure-all. Any problem you have can be resolved for a fleeting time by looking at pornography."

Remember, the emotional chaos your Inner Child experiences is extremely powerful and very frightening to him. Therefore, he requires an escape outlet that will serve to overpower his pain. That is where sex and pornography come in. The adrenaline rush provided by sexual behaviors is so effective it can help to mask any emotional distress.

How? By increasing the levels of dopamine and other neurochemicals in the brain. Dopamine, serotonin, and oxytocin are neurotransmitters the body naturally produces. However, addictive behaviors generate higher levels of these chemicals to create a rush or "high," similar to what is experienced when using cocaine and heroin.

SEEKING TRANSFORMATION

Once your Inner Child stumbles across this chemical method for easing his pain threshold, it is like leaving him alone in a candy store. He will want more. The key for us will be to stay **one step ahead** of the Child before his fear and meltdown kick in, sending us off running to obtain a neurochemical rush. To accomplish this, we will need to become more alert and mindful.

As men continue down the path of recovery, I encourage them to ponder the following question before making any decision. *"How will this action or inaction impact my wife and our marriage?"* This attitude is part of a new persona in which men learn to become more outwardly focused and aware of the needs and desires of others.

And it is the pathway God calls us to walk, challenging us to become better men. "And we all, who with unveiled faces contemplate the Lord's glory, are being transformed into his image with ever-increasing glory, which comes from the Lord, who is the Spirit" 2 Cor. 3:18.

Now understand this transformation approach flies in the face of the Inner Child's objective — *"I need to do whatever will help me feel safe and comfortable."* Can you see the potential problem?

THE INNER CHILD TAKES OVER

Let me take a moment to demonstrate how the Inner Child impacts us and our PSBs. I refer to this as the Inner Child Activation Process,

which results in the Child running the show and causing grief for us and those who love us.

Signs the Inner Child is Activated

Signs the Inner Child is activated. You may start to:
- Mood Shifts
- Anxiousness
- Fantasy
- Discomfort
- Intrusive Images/Thoughts
- Objectification of People
- Being Defiant
- Other Negative Emotions
- Seek to Sabotage
- Act Reckless

1. **Negative Event Occurs**
Could Occur Multiple Times a Day; may be Minor Events

2. **Inner Child Experiences Uncomfortable Emotions Correlated with Negative Event**
Inner Child has been Activated
Searches Emotional Warehouse for Past Events He Believes are Similar

3. **Inner Child Becomes Fearful**
- *Increases Your Anxiety and Discomfort*

4. **You Become Compulsive and Act Out**
- *Make the Wrong Decision to Escape Emotional Discomfort*

5. **You Experience Remorse**
- *Guilt and Shame*

Starting at the top of the diagram below, your troubles begin when negative events occur in your day-to-day life (Stage 1). These events could happen multiple times throughout the day, ranging from inconvenient to disastrous. In many cases, you may easily dismiss some of them. But there could be real trouble if the circumstances correlate with a core emotion trigger that haunts your Inner Child. Here is an example.

You are with your family at the shopping mall looking for a parking space. You see one, but just as you are about to pull in, another car cuts in front of you and grabs it (Stage 1). You are annoyed, but keep moving until you find another spot. Once in the mall with your wife and kids, you start shopping, trying not to think about the rude driver.

End of the story, right? Wrong. While you are attempting to dismiss the event, your Inner Child is not about to let the situation die. He has correlated the incident in the parking lot with bullying you endured in school and not standing up for yourself (Stage 2). Your Inner Child feels weak and humiliated, like when kids picked on you.

If you were to hear some of your Inner Child's negative self-talk, it would probably sound something like this. "Why didn't we do something when he cut us off? We never stood up to anyone in school. They would push us around and take our lunch money. We're weak and pathetic!" And there is your core emotional trigger – "I am weak."

THE INNER CHILD IN ACTION

When this occurs, your Inner Child is activated, which I assume you have concluded is not good. But how do you know the Child is starting to throw a tantrum? Easy. He wants to run away and forget about what happened. He wants to escape the emotional distress. So, what does he do? He engages in the same strategy he has been using for years. He makes you uncomfortable (box at left on the chart above). You may experience anxiousness, tension, irritability, numbness, anger, boredom, etc. And when you experience these troublesome feelings, you are programmed to seek out a distraction – which, in your case, usually involves sex.

Let us continue with our story at the mall. While you are unaware your Inner Child has been activated, your mood shifts, and your anxiety increases (Stage 3). You tell yourself you are getting tired and bored. But because you are not aware of your real emotions, you probably are not connecting the shift in mood to what happened in the parking lot. Instead, you may blame it on being at the mall when you could be home watching the football game. As your mood shifts downward, you tell your wife you need a break from shopping and that you are going to sit down.

After a few minutes, you start paying more attention to the women walking past (Stage 4). Being a "breast man," your eyes lock in on the many sizes of breasts—large, medium, and small.

You check out the breasts of every woman who passes one by one. You are lost in space and time and have forgotten where you are. You are dissociating. The only thing in your world now is the exploration and study of breasts.

Your Inner Child has achieved his objective. He is no longer focusing on the emotional turmoil that resulted from the parking lot incident and past bullies, while at the same time, he has prevented you from feeling weak. What a pal!

And the hunt for breasts has served as a significant distraction. Thanks to the rush of neurochemicals your brain is experiencing, you are in la-la land. Even your Inner Child has become quiet as you feast on the sights in the mall. And when your family finishes shopping and says they are ready to head home, you will not even know how long they have been gone.

The Inner Child Activation Process runs quietly in the background and can be kick-started numerous times during the day. The depth of your mood change can range from unnoticeable to dramatic depending on the event and the intensity with which it troubles your Inner Child. But it does not matter. If you are unaware of your Inner Child and his pain points, you will often be subjected to acting out when he is activated.

THE RUBBER BAND EFFECT

Here is an excellent word picture to better understand the power our unresolved childhood pain points have in creating dysfunction in our daily lives. The term *Rubber Band Effect* was created by Jeffrey Hollander, a licensed master social worker, to help explain to his clients the origin of their emotional triggers.

"The term describes what happens when, as adults, an emotion is triggered," Hollander said in explaining his concept. "The emotion snaps us back to what we experienced

lren, and we respond the same way we did as children,
's usually problematic.

"If you place a rubber band on your wrist, stretch it out, and then release it, it causes pains," he continued. "That's what happens to us emotionally when current events stir painful emotions from our past. The concept of a snapping rubber band helps clients understand what is occurring during those confusing and troubling times. Although they are no longer children, they continue to resort to coping strategies they used as children to numb their emotional distress. And those actions are usually destructive."

Again, Hollander's analogy concisely explains the Inner Child Activation Process and how we negatively react when our Inner Child is stirred up. It is also important to know that while our actions can be counterproductive, we resort to them to protect ourselves from experiencing subconscious emotional distress. What we require moving forward in managing our addictive behaviors is the development of new and healthy coping strategies.

The Inner Child in Action II

Let us look at another example of the Inner Child Activation Process, this time checking in on Bob after he receives a call from his boss, Cheryl, complaining about a project. (Note:

Bob is unaware of his Inner Child's dialogue that appears below.)

Bob: "Guess I will start reworking those numbers for Cheryl."

Bob's Inner Child: "I hate her. She is never happy and always complains about one thing or another. There is nothing we can do to make her happy."

Bob: "I thought I did a respectable job on that report."

Bob's Inner Child: "We're an idiot for trying to please her. No matter what we do, women like her will not be happy. She's just like Mom, who thought we were useless."

Bob: "Now that I think about it, she's not being fair." (Bob's anxiety is increasing.)

Bob's Inner Child: "We need to go to the massage parlor so we can experience what women are good for. We deserve that."

Bob: "I think I will take a break and go for a drive." (Compulsiveness kicks in.)

Can you imagine where Bob ended up? Yes, it is not hard to figure it out. But once his visit ends, he will beat himself up, wondering, *"How did I end up there?"* It proves his Inner

Child's enormous power heightens Bob's negative emotional state. While it is okay that Bob is upset with Cheryl, the intensity of his frustration increases because his Inner Child has added to the emotional distress by bringing Mom into the equation. And Bob is not consciously aware of what occurred. Let us review how this all played out.

Instead of recognizing the core emotional triggers that may result from Cheryl's call (*"I am not good enough"* and *"I am a disappointment"*) and then putting his effort into processing those emotions, Bob instead becomes a runner, following the lead of his Inner Child. He does not sit with the emotional pain caused by Cheryl's criticism but instead escapes to the massage parlor, a useful distraction until it ends.

Not understanding his Inner Child (or even realizing he has one) makes it impossible for Bob to slow down the Child. Therefore, Bob has yielded his power to his Inner Child without recognizing what he is doing. Side note – when you yield your power, you are heading off a cliff.

HIDING IN YOUR SUBCONSCIOUS

Unfortunately, most of us are unaware our Inner Child exists. And there is a good explanation, as Dr. Donald Price described in his article " *Inner Child Work: What is Really Happening?*

"The Inner Child is not just a visual image or metaphor, but a powerful and influential part of the self," explains Dr. Price. "However, the Inner Child may not be accessible through conscious exercises. The Inner Child is explained as a non-associated or dissociated and often disowned or disavowed part of the self or self-representation; it has some degree of ego-state formation and is state-dependent.

"It is a mental unit or structure of varying degrees of complexity or development, depending on the individual person, and often has the power to exert passive influence on the conscious state," continues Dr. Price.

Ok, that was heavy stuff. What the good doctor is saying is the Inner Child is buried in our subconscious; therefore, we are not aware of his presence, and because of this, he can create significant messes in our lives. Wow, that was easy!

You Need to Get to Know Your Inner Child and His Pain Points

Again, this does not make the Child bad. He is scared and confused and prone to react in emotionally charged ways. But there also is an incredibly positive aspect of our Inner Child. He can assist us in identifying our genuine emotions in any given circumstance.

Matt Price (no relation to the above Donald), in his book *Inner Child: Find Your True Self, Discover Your Inner Child, and Embrace the Fun in Life*, points out the positive nature of engaging our Inner Child.

"As we continued to mature, we learned to put on different masks or facades. We have learned to hide how we feel to avoid unpleasant encounters in life, such as pain, bitterness, rejection, and disappointment," says Price. "While these defense mechanisms do serve a healthy purpose to protect ourselves, we sometimes become detached from our true selves because of this fear. Sometimes these true feelings get bottled up and stowed away in some corner of your mind until they become so big that you will eventually burst and crack. The Inner Child can help you recover from this habit of holding it all in by letting you accept how you genuinely feel.

"For instance, many individuals have cheated on their partner because they hide their feelings of having 'fallen out of love.' They had to wait until they were tempted before they listened to their Inner Child, which has led them to inflict pain and sorrow upon another," he continues. "This would have been avoided if the person had acknowledged how he or she felt about his or her partner beforehand. The Inner Child can point out these true feelings and then enable the adult side to handle the situation maturely."

NOT KNOWING HE EXISTS IS OUR DOWNFALL

Our risk of acting inappropriately increases dramatically when we are unaware of the presence of our Inner Child and what core emotions are triggering him.

Dr. Stephen A. Diamond, authoring an article for Psychology Today entitled *Essential Secrets of Psychotherapy: The Inner Child,* points out that a triggered Inner Child can lead to chaos.

"We were all once children and still have that child dwelling within us. But most adults are quite unaware of this," said Dr. Diamond. "And this lack of conscious relatedness to our

Inner Child is precisely where so many behavioral, emotional, and relationship difficulties stem from."

Now, that is a crucial point made by Dr. Diamond you should not miss. Your Inner Child is a challenge because you are unaware of him. And that is a HUGE problem.

In fact, when it comes to our addictive behaviors, it is the biggest problem. Our lack of mindfulness regarding the little guy influences our downfall because we have been trained to follow his lead without asking questions. His actions were a defense mechanism created at a young age to deal with emotional turmoil.

"These so-called grown-ups or adults are unwittingly being constantly influenced or covertly controlled by this unconscious Inner Child," continues Dr. Diamond. "For many, it is not an adult self-directing their lives, but rather an emotionally wounded Inner Child inhabiting an adult body."

Are you starting to get the picture? You need to know your Inner Child, his fears, and what makes him want to escape. Believe it or not, learning about the Child and what makes him react in various situations is an exciting process.

The men I work with develop close-knit relationships with their Inner Children and often create nicknames to describe the kids.

"Dr. Eddie, you will not believe what little K tried to get away with this week," explained Kenny during one of his visits. "He is a handful, but I am working hard to stay one step ahead of him."

Working with your Child can be challenging because he has two goals: to avoid pain and seek stimulating pleasure. Neither of those are something a man struggling with PSBs should aim to accomplish.

TAKE A MOMENT: How can you relate to what you have read after this initial introduction to the Inner Child? Are you aware of the negative events you experience each day? Have you found yourself unaware of acting out until it is over? Again, this is called dissociation.

How Did the Kid Get This Way?

It is essential to briefly examine how our Inner Child developed into a fear-based kid. But first, let us review the conditions children MUST have to ensure healthy development.

- We need nurturing, and this includes attention and affirmation. As children, we long to be wanted and desired. Knowing we are loved and that someone is there for us is critical. This sense of belonging is vital in developing healthy self-worth.

- We need structure. We require rules and discipline. Now, you may be saying that is ridiculous; kids want to do what they want to do. Yes and no. When our parents provide us with structure, we feel valued. They are providing us with the guidance and protection we need to survive.

- We need protection. Children do not have the skills to deal with emotional distress (anxiety). They do not have enough worldly experiences, and their thought process is more emotionally based than cognitively based. That being said, when a child is distressed, if there is no one he can turn to for guidance, he produces one solution to resolve his dilemma – *"I won't think about it."* How does he accomplish this? He finds distractions—too much television, sugar, food, fantasy, etc. What activity he selects is unimportant as long as it quiets his anxiety. Not knowing, the child has set the stage for his adult life where he will seek to avoid negative emotions using what will ultimately be destructive behaviors for him and his relationships. His running, over time, becomes a compulsion (insatiable urge). Compulsions can turn into addictions (dependency).

- We need stimulation. A child's brain is like a sponge that craves interaction and knowledge. It is natural for children to seek adventure and excitement to help develop curiosity and a sense of autonomy. When a child is not stimulated or challenged to explore and learn because of neglectful parents, his intellectual and emotional growth becomes stifled. Basically, no one teaches us how to live and love. Instead, we simply exist.

When a child is denied developmental growth in one or more of these areas, he will experience uncertainty and anxiety, leading to a frightened Inner Child. A lack of nurturing will lead a child to question his value and self-worth. Since he is not being loved and affirmed, he will see himself as the problem and believe he is unlovable.

Being egocentric, children have difficulty blaming parents who do not demonstrate love and affection. A child cannot see a situation from another person's point of view; therefore, they assume others feel the same. So, in a child's mind, there is only one explanation for why mommy and daddy do not love on me — *"There is something wrong with me."*

In his book, *Homecoming: Reclaiming and Healing Your Inner Child,* John Bradshaw discussed how the Inner Child's identity is hindered by wounds afflicted during the early years.

"The wounded Inner Child contaminates intimacy in relationships because he has no sense of his authentic self," says Bradshaw, whose book is considered one of the best works to describe the Inner Child. "The greatest wound a child can receive is the rejection of his authentic self. When a parent cannot affirm his child's feelings, needs, and desires, he rejects that child's authentic self. Then, a false self must be set up."

Without structure, children do not feel secure or develop the ability to master self-discipline (does that sound like you?). Parents who set up routines for their children communicate the message, *"I care, and you are important. You can feel safe with me."*

When no structure surrounds a child, he deals with a fear of the unknown. This lack of structure is terrifying for kids who live with uncertainty and do not know what to expect day by day.

Lack of structure also prevents children from learning to discipline themselves. Since there are few rules, and it seems no one cares, why should the child? Worst yet, this child is more likely not to reflect upon the consequences of his actions. This makes it more likely he will engage in risky behavior. Oh, wait, that sounds like someone dealing with PSBs!

And there is another negative impact that results from a lack of consistent parenting. Since the child grows up believing no one cares, he must take it upon himself to provide his own caring and nurturing. This results in him turning inward and looking out for himself first. Because if he does not, who will?

OUR LOW EMOTIONAL IQ

When we lack stimulation as children, we are set up for failure as adults. Being deprived of various sensory stimulation limits brain development. And nowhere is the lack of stimulation more relevant than in the underdevelopment of an individual's emotional IQ. In my clinical practice, 9 out of 10 men who present with PSBs also have an extremely low emotional IQ. What this means is three-fold.

1. They can tell you when they are angry, sad, happy, lonely, or afraid. These are called primary or instinctive emotions. However, they struggle to identify their genuine emotions, which are called secondary emotions. For example, they exhibit anger, but the real emotion driving the anger may be feeling disrespected.

2. If they can identify true feelings (secondary emotions), they cannot constructively articulate them. They struggle to share because of the fear of being dismissed or belittled. They consider vulnerability a dirty word.

3. But worst of all, they cannot determine what others feel beyond primary emotions. They cannot empathize and seek additional information from others expressing their feelings because the emotions bring anxiety. Instead, they seek to shut

down the individual, fix the problem, or minimize it — all to reduce their anxiety.

Beyond PSBs, a low emotional IQ is the most significant complaint women have about the men in their lives – they lack the ability to connect emotionally. I tell couples most of these men would not know emotional intimacy if it hit them in the face. This is not a

criticism of men; I too had an extremely low emotional IQ when I started my recovery work. A low emotional IQ serves as a harmful component in manifesting our PSBs. We do not allow ourselves to feel to escape emotional distress. But what this leads to is an inability to feel much at all. You cannot cut off bad emotions without limiting your positive emotions.

While your Inner Child experiences emotions (a vast majority being painful), he does not know how to process them or self-soothe himself. Because he was never taught how to manage his negative feelings successfully, he chooses not to feel them by developing distractions (running away).

In her book *Running on Empty*, Dr. Jonice Webb points out how children suffering from neglect learn to cut off their emotions to protect themselves and how it results in them becoming adults with low emotional IQs.

"When you grow up with your parents failing to notice what you are feeling, you are growing up with the most powerful expression of your deepest self (your emotions) ignored. What is a child to do?" she writes. "Fortunately, and unfortunately, children's brains automatically step in to protect them in these situations. When, as a child, you perceive, on some level, that your emotions are not welcome in your family, your brain automatically walls them off for you. This way, those troublesome feelings won't burden you and your parents. In many ways, this coping technique is brilliantly adaptive. But it's also what makes you feel empty as an adult."

> ## MEN STRUGGLING WITH PSBS
> ## MUS UNDERSTAND THE CONCEPT OF
> ## "YOU NEED TO FEEL TO HEAL"

The inability to deal with negative feelings and engage in real emotional intimacy leads men to spiral out of control into relational dysfunction.

"Growing up and moving forward in your life, you are unaware of what your brain has done for you," Dr. Webb continues. "You are not aware of your blocked feelings. You are unaware that you are living your life without full access to a key life ingredient that everyone else has: your emotions."

You can learn more about the lack of childhood development skills and its impact on individuals and relationships in my book, *Why Men Struggle to Love: Overcoming Relational Blind Spots*.

THE DEVASTATING IMPACT OF THE INNER CHILD

As mentioned before, being unaware of your Inner Child and his core emotional triggers is like walking blindfolded on the streets of Manhattan. Eventually, you will hit something, or something will hit you.

Dr. Charles Whitfield, the author of *Healing the Child Within*, writes the inability to understand what triggers our Inner Children can lead to severe consequences, causing deep emotional and mental distress.

"When the child within is not nurtured or allowed freedom of expression, a false or co-dependent self emerges," he says. "We begin to live our lives from a victim stance and experience difficulties in resolving emotional traumas. The gradual accumulation of unfinished mental and emotional business can lead to chronic anxiety, fear, confusion, emptiness, and unhappiness."

YOUR INNER CHILD CAN RECALL MESSAGES YOU RECEIVED, DIRECTLY AND INDIRECTLY, THAT HARMED YOU EMOTIONALLY AND MENTALLY

What Dr. Whitfield does not explain is this *unfinished business* we experience can lead our Inner Child to seek out behaviors – such as PSBs – to escape emotional pain.

Dr. Esly Carvalho agrees the Inner Child connects to our past trauma and neglect, much of which we have erased from our conscious thought process.

"Unhealed traumatic experiences eternally repeat themselves inside of us. This repetition doesn't end because the brain stays actively connected to our unprocessed memories," according to Dr. Carvalho's book, Healing the

Folks Who Live Inside. "Our brain stays in a state of hypervigilance because the deep brain continues to feel the need to protect itself from perceived danger. It is as if our mind does not 'know' the danger has passed, so it continues in high alert, in an anxious state, always concerned that something bad is going to happen. Somebody inside continues to live and relive the traumatic experience."

As I pointed out earlier, your Inner Child is locked in a time warp. He is trapped forever in those years when you endured trauma/neglect that left suppressed emotional scars. However, your Inner Child knows every imperfection intimately. He can recall messages you received directly and indirectly from parents, siblings, peers, and other authority figures that harmed you emotionally and mentally. The Child has memorized every negative narrative you have taught yourself. He forgets nothing. Even though you have.

NEGATIVE NARRATIVES

Negative narratives (or negative self-talk) are unfavorable beliefs you inflict upon yourself. They play ever-so-softly in your mind; often, you can barely hear them. The following are examples of some negative narratives:

> **YOU DO NOT DESERVE LOVE**
> **YOU ARE A BAD PERSON**
> **YOU ARE WORTHLESS**
> **YOU ARE NOT LOVABLE**
> **YOU ARE POWERLESS**
> **YOU ARE INVISIBLE**

YOU ARE NOT GOOD ENOUGH
YOU ARE A MISTAKE
YOU ARE ALWAYS WRONG
YOU ARE UGLY/UNATTRACTIVE
YOU ARE STUPID
YOU DO NOT BELONG
YOU ARE A FAILURE
YOU ARE A DISAPPOINTMENT
YOU ARE DEFECTIVE

These are only a handful of the destructive lies we learned to believe about ourselves at the hands of the people and events that hard-wired us as children. When a negative event occurs in our daily lives, it may remind the Inner Child of a negative narrative, which will cause him to be triggered.

For example, one of your co-workers, Stan, walks right by you in the hallway without saying hello (Stage 1). You find it curious because Stan is one of the friendliest guys in the company, but you tell yourself he was probably distracted.

However, your Inner Child is not taking the same rational approach to sort out what happened with Stan. He immediately recalls previous times when others ignored you (Stage 2).

"I remember when Tommy turned everyone against us in third grade, and we didn't do anything wrong. The other kids walked by us and didn't talk to us for the last six weeks of the school year. We felt left out. You can't trust people who say they like you!"

Your Inner Child has had years to replay the traumas and neglects you endured as a kid. Because of this, he is fear-driven and reactive. He relies solely on emotional thinking to deal with the circumstances you face today and often misreads them, ultimately

causing unnecessary emotional and mental distress.

Go back to Stan for a moment. You are sitting at your desk and cannot concentrate because you feel Stan is upset with you – that you have done something wrong (Step 3). But a moment later, he pops his head in your office and says, *"Want to hit the cafeteria for a cup of coffee?"* Stan's actions have cut short the activation cycle, and your risk of acting out has been dramatically reduced.

Stan may have triggered your Inner Child by not acknowledging you, but the Child's conclusion was wrong. That is what happens when we react, using only our emotional-focused thinking.

TAKE A MOMENT: What negative narratives play in your head? How do you believe they may have originated?

Our Inner Child is driven by emotional thinking because, as a child, it was the most advanced thinking skill he had available when facing a crisis and conflict. His analytical and cognitive capabilities were not fully developed, leaving him to make assumptions based on raw emotions and limited worldly experiences.

He had limited use of critical, analytical, or concrete thinking skills that we as adults utilize to assist us in assessing troubling situations. He was – and still is – alone and in the dark, trying to navigate a world he does not fully understand, which often brings more pain and uncertainty than pleasure.

As you can imagine, his perception of things may not match reality because of this dilemma. He is a highly reactive fellow who runs on impulsiveness. It is strictly a reactive urge to act without thinking of further consequences. In fact, he believes his course of action — escape and seek adrenaline rushes — will bring about pleasurable results. Unfortunately for us, he is wrong.

IT IS ABOUT PAST PAIN

In his book Unwanted, Jay Stringer points out that PSBs are created through the entanglement of two worlds. "How did I get here?" he writes. "One way of thinking about unwanted sexual behavior is to see it as the convergence of two rivers: your past and the difficulties you face in the present."

Consider your Inner Child's river (your past) muddy and dreary to take his brilliant word picture to the next level. When he overreacts to current events happening today — your river — his highly reactive nature starts to pollute your water. All the mud and debris from past emotional pain comes roaring into your current river, leaving you dealing with negative feelings, increased anxiety, and, worst yet, not understanding how everything turned chaotic. You see, your Inner Child is responsible for informing you an event has occurred that will change your mood (and not for the better). To him, current circumstances may seem strikingly identical to past traumas and neglect, and he has been triggered.

In turn, your level of discomfort increases — although you may not be aware of it at the time. The current negative event may have increased your anxiety level to a three (based on a scale of 0 to 10). However, after your Inner Child drags in a past pain point he believes is similar to the current event, your anxiety level may escalate, perhaps to an eight or nine.

The more your anxiety increases, the greater your risk of being compulsive. And with great compulsiveness comes an increased risk of poor decision-making. (Again, refer to the Inner Child Activation Process Chart to better understand this process.)

THE INNER CHILD AND HARRY

Let us look at another example. Harry and three other members of his design team are called to the boardroom by the company CEO, who announces they have won a new client thanks to their hard work. Not intentionally, when the group gathers, three team members sit on one side of the table, and Harry sits alone on the other side. In talking with the team, the CEO looks at Harry's counterparts, praising and affirming. Realizing he has left Harry out, he turns to him and, with a slight grin, says, *"You did a good job, too"* (Stage 1). Harry nods and smiles. But something is wrong.

INCREASED ANXIETY LEADS TO…
INCREASED COMPULSIVENESS THAT LEADS TO…
POOR DECISION MAKING

The CEO's glance and grin toward Harry caused "Little Harold" (the name of Harry's Inner Child) to experience the emotional pain of being minimized and unnoticed. Little Harold feels like an afterthought.

As the CEO speaks, Little Harold immediately remembers when Dad told Harry's twin brother, Larry, how proud he was for driving in the winning run during a Little League game. Although Harry had three hits that game, Dad looked at him and grinned quickly before turning his attention back to Larry. It probably was not his father's intention to slight Harry, but that is what happened. And it occurred on more than one occasion. Harry often felt he played second banana to Larry when it came to Dad's affirmation and attention.

"I was never as good as Larry," Little Harold recalls as the meeting goes on. "Dad loved him better. And I know why. It was because I was a good athlete. I just wasn't good enough. I was never good enough." (Stage 2). Harry's Inner Child is full of negative self-talk, and because of it, Harry is about to suffer.

As Harry left the meeting, he forgot the situation and briefly celebrated the win with his peers, but for some reason, he was not in the mood to celebrate (Stage 3). Instead, he justified his mood by telling himself it was no big deal to win a new client and that he needed to get back to work, which he did.

Later, he stopped at a massage parlor (Stage 4) and allowed a woman to masturbate him. Feeling disgusted after it was over (Stage 5), he wondered why on the ride home. It had been months since the last time, and he told himself, *"Never again."* What Harry did not know was Little Harold was running the show.

What did Harry do wrong that led to his poor decision-making? First, he did not slow everything down to recognize the mood shift he was experiencing after the CEO's comments. He had two opportunities to do this.

1. During the meeting, after he received the "glance"

2. At the celebration, he found himself not in the mood to participate with his co-workers

Harry's lack of mindfulness about his shifting emotional state proved a careless mistake that left him feeling shameful. Again, mindfulness is critical to the recovery process. Without it, you will struggle repeatedly.

TAKE A MOMENT: Based on what you have been learning, how does your Inner Child impact your PSBs? Can you identify some of your potential core emotional triggers?

Is it not interesting to see the correlation between your Inner Child's mindset and your behavior regarding your PSBs? Both of you are:

- Feeling some level of emotional discomfort (anxiety)
- Being compulsive
- Not focused on potential consequences
- Trying to escape emotional distress and seek comfort

Yep, having an Inner Child in charge of the show causes mental and emotional pain and grief. That is why we must become empowered.

HE IS NOT GOING ANYWHERE

I have had clients ask me, *"When does the child leave me alone?"* The answer is never. Your Inner Child is not going away. The pain he feels does not diminish much over time. But he can be taught to adapt.

The more you work to help comfort, teach, and protect, the more the Child will learn to trust you and your course of action. Mainly, he wants to know if there is an adult in charge who can handle the discomfort he is facing. That is something he lacked growing up. No one was there to explain his emotional pain and provide comfort and reassurance. Moving forward, you will be that adult.

He will still be activated when a core emotional trigger occurs, but you will find it easier to get his attention and allow him to give up control of the situation, therefore permitting you to take charge. You will then be staying one step ahead of him and your PSBs.

But it is an ongoing process. The more you become mindful of your PSBs, your Inner Child, and his core emotional triggers, the greater success you will experience in managing difficult situations as they arise. Mindfulness is a significant component of the recovery process, which we will cover in-depth later.

Remember, we are not trying to discipline or shame our Inner Child. He cannot control his emotions because he is stuck in a period where he experiences tremendous emotional, mental, and perhaps physical distress. No one helped him learn how to deal with stressful situations. Therefore, based on his limited life experiences, he had to sort through his trauma and neglect alone.

Imagine being six to 14 years old and trying to determine why dad does not pay attention to you. No one is available to help you sort through the pain, hurt, and disappointment you feel. In most cases, you wind up taking responsibility, thinking there is something wrong with you, and that is the reason why Daddy is ignoring you.

Getting in tune with your Inner Child results in deepening your self-awareness, which the Child lacks. This new skill set will allow you to stay alert of high-risk situations, while also assisting you in comforting your Inner Child. By doing this, you will learn to manage your PSBs.

THE INNER CHILD AND PARTNERS

Does the Inner Child lead the addicted spouse to withhold love from the betrayed spouse? No, while in 90% of cases, the addicted partner is emotionally undeveloped and does not understand the meaning of emotional intimacy, his Inner Child is desperate to experience love and acceptance. However, the Child also does not understand how to engage in an emotionally intimate relationship, usually not seeing the model as a child.

Also, the spouse's grieving leaves the Inner Child fearful. He does not understand betrayal trauma and only sees anger and hostility thrown in his direction. This conflict often reminds him of other past individuals who also scared him. Therefore, he is reluctant to seek comfort from his spouse and instead will elect to become aggressive or isolate.

The Child will resort to blaming, gaslighting, aggression, and withdrawal when interacting with the spouse whenever he feels threatened and afraid. He immediately wants to shut down the hostility he believes is aimed at him and reminds him of similar circumstances he experienced as a child.

So, what do betrayal spouses do when their husbands' Inner Children attempt to get involved in conversations? I tell women to do the following: express how you feel about the current situation and how your husband is acting. Tell him you believe his Inner Child is activated and involved in the discussion. And then take this important step – walk away.

This action will stop him in his tracks, and he will begin to self-reflect, trying to understand how the Child is causing you emotional pain. Do not be surprised if he comes looking for you to apologize.

Never allow your Inner Child to speak with your spouse is one of my 10 rules for engaging with your grieving partner.

And it is one of the most important rules. How can you tell if your Inner Child is speaking with your spouse? You are most likely defensive, argumentative, and whiny. Your conversation will sound like a that of a child. Another way you can tell if your Inner Child is speaking to your spouse is she will be extremely angry.

FIVE OBJECTIVES

As we finish Chapter 2 and prepare to meet the 12 kids, first, let us briefly review five points I want you to remember when reading the rest of this book.

1. Become aware of your Inner Child. Start the process of understanding what he has gone through and his fears. Learn to have empathy for him despite the havoc he can cause. He is not a bad child. He is scared.

2. Identify and understand his core emotional triggers to limit how they negatively impact you. Many core emotional triggers could activate an Inner Child and push you toward acting out to maintain control over anxiety. That is why it is essential to determine what core emotional triggers activate your Child. That is accomplished partly by examining the cast of characters and events that negatively influenced your life. Remember this: it is not the children you select that are the most essential element of this model, it is the core emotional triggers that activate the children you select.

3. Learn how to educate, comfort, and protect your Inner Child. He must understand that an adult is

willing to guide him, and he does not have to try to manage the scary situation alone. He also must learn to understand that today's circumstances do not always correlate with suffering from the past. It just seems that way. What he feels and what is real are usually two different things. That last sentence is especially important; you will see it again as you read.

4. Stop running away from the emotional pain impacting your Inner Child and instead learn to sit with hurtful emotions. This is a challenging step. We have programmed ourselves to avoid emotional pain at all costs. But running away and trying to escape reality is no longer an option. Nothing good comes from turning away from your fears. Confronting our pain offers real benefits, including helping us mature.

5. Although the Child has enormous power and influence, YOU are still responsible for your decision-making. And that will only happen when you decide to take control and become more mindful of yourself, your Inner Child, and your surroundings.

What are your initial thoughts about the concept of the Inner Child? Do you feel optimistic or pessimistic about the pending journey you are entering? Why?

_____

_____

_____

_____

_____

_____

_____

_____

_____

_____

_____

_____

_____

HEADS UP: As we move along, I will be sharing the Inner Child Model™ for Treating PSBs that will provide you with the ultimate solution for managing your Inner Child when he becomes activated and staying one step ahead of your addictive behaviors. But now, let us meet the 12 Inner Children.

CHAPTER 3
Meet the Kids and Their Troubling Fears

"Triggers are like little psychic explosions that crash through our avoidance and bring the dissociated, avoided trauma suddenly, unexpectedly, back into consciousness."

– Carolyn Spring, Author

Through research conducted over the years in my practice, I have uncovered 12 of the most common rationales (my Inner Children) for why men abuse sex. The interesting aspect regarding these rationales is only one has anything to do with sex.

NEVER STOP QUESTIONING WHY

As you start this process of internal self-reflection, it is important to note each Inner Child has a unique emotional pain point that has gone unresolved and still haunts you today. It is also important to know not all negative emotions will impact your Inner Child. The goal is to identify the core emotional triggers that lead to your Child's tantrums. With this insight, you will develop the tools to reduce your anxiety and lower your risk of acting out compulsively.

These 12 Inner Children have unique core emotional triggers based on their pain points. For example, the Unnoticed Child deals with the following core emotional triggers:

- I do not matter
- I do not belong
- I am forgotten
- I have been dismissed
- I am ignored
- I am invisible

Part of your self-reflection will be determining which core emotional triggers generate the most discomfort (mental, emotional, physical) when you experience them.

Finally, the following descriptions in this chapter are only brief overviews of each Inner Child. We will review every child in-depth throughout the rest of this book. As you read, highlight, or journal about the children who resonate most with you. Note that each child's description may not match up entirely with what you experienced growing up. That is okay. The point is to identify children who seem to touch a raw nerve and make you uncomfortable. Let the quest for insight begin!

THE BORED CHILD

 I cannot begin to tell you how many men I have counseled who resonate with this Child. With the explosion of technology and numerous ways to entertain and stimulate ourselves, individuals are growing up believing they need to do something 24/7. Any downtime seems like wasted time. But having endless entertainment options at our fingertips is insufficient to overcome boredom. The antidote to boredom is healthy relationships.

Men who associate with this Child were often raised in environments that offered little positive interaction and stimulation with family members. Even if they came from a large family surrounded by people, they often felt isolated and alone. Some were latch-key children. As young boys, they grew up learning to entertain themselves, which led them to spend a lot of time in their heads while strengthening their fantasy-development muscles.

They may have had no or few friends and spent a great deal of this time alone, engaging in fantasy and self-play. They often felt like outcasts and not accepted by their peers. These men led a low-key and quiet existence as children and teenagers. And this is a critical point – their lives lacked authentic and healthy stimulation. The stimulation they required was positive and healthy engagement with other people.

Then, one day, these young boys experience a great awakening. They stumble upon sex. This exposes them to a stimulation level like they had never felt before. They find sex captivating and exhilarating. Their attention is laser-focused on sex as they find ways to feed their newfound desire.

With sex, life is anything but boring. Young girls are no longer seen as potential playmates but now as playthings. Dreaded time spent alone is now welcomed as an opportunity to fantasize, objectify girls and boys, and masturbate.

THE BORED CHILD OFTEN WILL COME TO BELIEVE 'NO ONE CARES' ABOUT HIM

The stimulant of sex is hypnotizing. And over time, these boys need more sex to keep boredom at bay.

Why? Because the same sexual images or activities become old and dull. Stagnant sex no longer has the power and ability to manufacture neurochemicals – especially dopamine – at a satisfying level.

That is why men who are hooked do not seek more – they seek different. It is also why they become enslaved to PSBs.

"I can recall a time when just looking at a picture of a naked woman was enough to arouse me," said Curtis, a 46-year-old married father of two who has struggled with pornography since he was 11. "But over the years, the videos I watched had to be more intense and disturbing for me to get sexually excited. I think back at some of the content I was viewing, and it makes me nauseous."

As an adult, this individual is now programmed to fill dull and quiet moments with the quest to obtain the chemical rush sex delivers. The emotional pain of boredom or *"no one cares about me"* can be quieted through various sexual activities ranging from masturbation to engaging a prostitute. The Inner Child has come to understand with sex, there is never a dull moment.

THE UNNOTICED CHILD

One of the keys to developing healthy children is providing them with a sense of belonging. A child's understanding that he is accepted and desired is vital in creating solid ego strength and confidence. But that is not how life plays out for boys who go through childhood and adolescence, never feeling they belong. In some cases, they had to chase friends and family members to be included and recognized. These children were rarely sought out by others and often wondered, *"what's wrong with me that someone would not go through the trouble of finding me?"*

Others were "drowned" out by family members or peers and grew up feeling they had no voice. It would not be uncommon for them to make comments that were totally ignored or glanced over at the dinner table. This lack of attention made them feel invisible or small.

Like the Bored Child, these Inner Children spent much time isolated. They were left alone with their thoughts, ideas, and worries, reluctant to share for fear of being dismissed or belittled. They developed an intense fear of rejection, which would keep them from taking risks in reaching out to others for engagement. One of their worldviews is *"it's safer to go it alone."*

I find this especially true of clients who report being bullied. In fact, a high percentage of my clients, more than 75%, report being bullied as a child and teenager. Of course, this type of trauma only increases the likelihood of children withdrawing and isolating, thus reinforcing the feeling they are not desired or wanted.

Today, the Inner Child of this man still craves to belong. He is hungry for others to pursue him and make him feel desired. That is why this guy may be in a relationship where his partner is very attentive, but it is not enough to make him feel content. His need to be desired is so strong that whatever attention he may receive from his wife may not be satisfying enough. Therefore, he is compelled to seek additional attention from others in a hopeless attempt to satisfy his bottomless emotional deficiency.

BULLYING INCREASES THE LIKELIHOOD A CHILD WILL FEEL UNDESIRED OR UNWANTED

"Cindy is amazing at making me feel special," said Andy about his wife of 16 years. Andy struggles as a womanizer and has had numerous affairs during his marriage. His mother suffered from depression and isolated a great deal, which left Andy feeling abandoned and unloved. Despite being a handsome guy, he had never dated before meeting Cindy. *"I was always shy, so I did not seek out or approach girls. Because I was socially awkward, kids teased me a lot. I feared being around people because I felt I didn't fit in. It sucks when no one wants to be your friend."*

As adults, men like Andy do not always aggressively seek women's attention; however, they may struggle to walk away if a woman expresses interest in them. *"I wasn't looking for relationships or affair partners,"* Andy explained. *"But I couldn't hold back when women started flirting with me. I didn't even think about my wife or kids. My sole focus was on how comforting it felt to be with them. It was like I had no control."*

What went wrong for Andy? You got it. His Inner Child was running the show. His Child believes Andy's attention from his wife will not last, and he will again be abandoned.

Unfortunately for Andy, one of his affair partners was his wife's best friend. Her flirting turned into a year-long affair that ended his marriage. Andy did not have a chance because he was unaware of his Inner Child and the hunger for attention the Child demanded. Because of this lack of awareness, Andy was like a moth drawn to a flame when women came calling. He did not want sex. He wanted attention.

Believe it or not, the quest for attention can be fulfilled through pornography. When viewing porn, men drift off into a fantasy that fulfills a sense of being wanted. I have heard many men admit they obtain a feeling of being desired when watching porn and seeing the smiling faces of women, which they find so inviting.

Men who engage with prostitutes, strippers, or online video escorts also fantasize that these women hunger for them. *"I know it's not true in my head,"* says Robert. *"But when I am with an escort, it is my fantasy that she only wants me. I know it sounds stupid, but it gives me a great deal of validation that someone wants to spend time with me even if I am paying for it."*

THE UNAFFIRMED CHILD

Imagine growing up and never or rarely hearing your parents or others say things like:

"That was an impressive job."

"You're an amazing kid."

"I think you're special."

"You're very smart."

"I enjoy spending time with you."

"I am so proud of you."

"You're fun to be with."

"I love you."

That is the issue facing an Inner Child who is hungry for praise. This Child was raised in an environment where he received little affirmation and/or probably over-the-top criticism. It left him feeling nothing he did was good enough and wondering, *"what's wrong with me?"*

Growing up receiving few accolades – and perhaps a great deal of criticism – leads to the development of low self-worth and a lack of confidence. These young boys rarely had their achievements acknowledged, or worse yet, they were told many times their efforts fell short. Even if they obtained success through academics or athletics, they believed their accomplishments were tainted or meaningless.

PORN CAN PROVIDE MEN WITH A PSEUDO-FEELING OF AFFIRMATION

Since they cannot escape criticism, they turn to fantasy to create a world where they are always affirmed. Like the child who craves attention, this kid fantasizes about receiving praise from the women he sees when flipping through pages in a porn magazine or watching a video. These women are secure, inviting, and friendly. The Inner Child learns there is no rejection found in viewing pornography.

Another situation responsible for the development of Unaffirmed Children is receiving tremendous and continuous accolades for their academic or athletic performances or appearance. Now, they crave affirmation that is difficult to find once the spotlight went out.

"They were safe and friendly," explained Bennett as he recalled engaging with Internet video chat, where he paid women to strip for him. "I always felt as though they were doing it because they thought I was special and wanted to please only me." You can hear Bennett's Inner Child longing for comfort in that quote. But he was looking in the wrong place.

It is not only porn that provides an outlet for affirmation. Many men get similar thrills in trolling social media. They scroll through the faces and profiles of women and men while fantasizing about the appreciation and admiration they could receive from individuals they do not know.

"My wife was so annoyed when she caught me surfing her Facebook page and looking at profiles of the women she was friends with," said Lyndon, who struggles with pornography and online chat. "I was so embarrassed when I finally admitted to her why I was doing it. She called me a freak and blocked me from her Facebook page."

These fantasies provide great comfort – the Inner Child's number one desire – but there is one problem: the affirmation is not real. It may offer a temporary buzz, but these guys come crashing back to earth again as their Inner Child asks, *what's wrong with me?*

Although they are chasing affirmation, these men are often hypersensitive to criticism. Because of their sensitivity to being corrected, the praise they receive is never enough.

With every positive comment they receive, a keen ear is listening for the criticism they are sure will follow. Their spouses often complain these men are oversensitive and tend to withdraw and pout when someone is upset with them.

For this Child, seeking praise is a bottomless cup that never gets filled. It leads to engaging in an endless search for approval and recognition, which comes with destructive consequences.

THE EMOTIONALLY VOIDED CHILD

Like the kid who received little or no affirmation, some children are raised in an environment where emotions are shunned, like COVID-19. Sure, there were expressions of anger, sadness, happiness, loneliness, and fear, but deep-rooted feelings were off-limits—a no-no. These kids grow up with no model of what it is like to bond with other people emotionally. No one shows them how to identify, process, and share their feelings in a healthy manner. Instead, they are left alone to figure out how to deal with the emotional pain of scarring events.

Along the way, they received the message that *"feelings are not important – and perhaps dangerous to share."* To protect himself, this Inner Child decides to stop feeling. He becomes proficient at suppressing emotions and locking them away in a black box so they can never be reached.

The result? An emotionally undeveloped adult who has no idea how to bond emotionally with others. He has no clue what emotional intimacy entails and, therefore, cannot connect in a healthy way with others.

"I always thought emotional intimacy was telling someone you loved them or having sex," said Hunter, 32, who has been addicted to pornography since discovering it at 13. "But now I know emotional intimacy is much deeper and requires me to be open and vulnerable. To tell you the truth, although I practice being vulnerable, it's still frightening to share my feelings. I'm always worried I will be dismissed."

The emotionally undeveloped guy may be uncomfortable in social or family settings for an extended period. He prefers to keep to himself or latches onto one individual to reduce his anxiety in social situations. I often hear these clients express their frustration of not knowing what to discuss with others.

"I hated social events because I always struggled to think of topics to discuss with people," said Hunter. "I will sit and listen but do not know what to say."

The word picture I provide of an emotionally undeveloped man is racing through life with his head down. In doing so, he cannot observe what is happening around him. His Inner Child wants to maintain a low profile, hoping not to be noticed – *"don't call on me!"*

As mentioned, these men find it challenging to identify and express their core emotions except for anger, sadness, happiness, loneliness, and fear. Still, worse yet, they struggle to connect with the feelings of others. This leads people to think of them as aloof and distant. The real problem is they are not very observant about their surroundings and others. And that is a common complaint from partners — *"he's in the room, but he may as well be miles away."*

THEIR INNER CHILD WANTS TO MAINTAIN A LOW PROFILE IN HOPES OF NOT BEING NOTICED – "DON'T CALL ON ME!"

"My wife has always complained I am not available to her and the kids," said Jackson, who suffered from pornography addiction. "Looking back, I guess she was right to complain. For some reason, I enjoy going off by myself and being alone. Engaging with anyone for more than 15 minutes is emotionally and mentally exhausting.

"But with pornography, it is different," he continued. "Somehow, I feel emotionally connected with the people in the videos. I can't explain it, but it makes me feel alive."

What men like Jackson are experiencing is pseudo-intimacy, which is non-threatening because the other participants ask nothing of them. Like other men who struggle with PSBs, Jackson utilizes fantasy that alters his brain chemistry, which creates the "alive" buzz he feels.

The bottom line is these men confuse sex and physical touch with emotional intimacy. They believe sex is the pathway to emotional connection and bonding. It would be okay if they mixed other forms of emotional intimacy into their relationships. These guys cannot. And that can leave partners feeling used.

THE NEED FOR CONTROL CHILD

If you like chaos, raise your hand. No takers, uh? Most people do not like being surrounded by turmoil and drama. However, for many young boys, that is precisely the environment they were raised in. Their homes were habitats of disorder and, in some cases, mayhem.

Some were emotionally, mentally, physically, or sexually abused. Others suffered from neglect. And in some cases, they were raised in an anxious environment where the home never seemed inviting. Whatever conditions they faced, the backdrop included anxiety. And with all the confusion these young boys experienced, they came to understand one critical point – they lacked the power to change things. As a result, they were stuck like animals in a cage, having to endure whatever came their way.

Welcome to the jungle.

Today, all grown up, these men are driven by their Inner Children, who are control freaks. Why? Because as the past demonstrated, when a situation is out of control, they suffer the consequences. Therefore, by taking control of circumstances and others, the Inner Child believes he is preventing bad things from occurring. Of course, that is the furthest thing from the truth. Their controlling nature often leads to increased anxiety for themselves and those around them.

For these men, their Inner Children also have learned to rely on sex to establish control. How is this control? Sex serves as a distraction from day-to-day negative events and stressful emotions. They learn to use sex as a diversion to lower anxiety and keep emotional distress at bay. Over time, they lean on sex to combat any anxious scenario they cannot control. Like all men who deal with PSBs, they learn to run away from their emotional and mental tribulations. Sex becomes an effortless way to manage the unmanageable and provides a pseudo sense of power.

But not all boys who use sex to distract from things they cannot control were raised in chaotic households. Some dealt with parents who were micromanagers. These young men were given little in the way of freedom to make their own choices. It would not be uncommon for parents and older siblings to point out how these children consistently did things incorrectly. This left these kids feeling unsure about themselves and often frustrated. As adults, they overcome this frustration by not relinquishing control and perhaps becoming perfectionists.

BY TAKING CONTROL OF EVENTS AND OTHERS, THE INNER CHILD BELIEVES HE IS PREVENTING BAD THINGS FROM HAPPENING

"With pornography, I can enjoy sex anytime and anyway I want," said Ethan, who was fired after being caught watching pornography at work. He was a military brat whose father ruled with an iron fist. There were a lot of rules and no room

for mistakes. *"I never made a single decision on my own until I went to college. And one of those decisions was to start watching porn. It was exciting because I felt like I called the shots, and women would indulge in any form of sexual activity I desired."*

As we discussed before, this is not a reality, but for the Inner Child who requires control to feel safe, pseudo-control is real enough.

THE ENTITLED-SPITEFUL CHILD

It is not unusual for toddlers to *"want what they want."* The natural selfishness of humanity is on display in young children's youthfulness and innocence. Fortunately, a vast majority of us grow out of this mindset and learn to be patient, understanding, and how to share.

This Child does not get upset because he thinks he is better than anyone else, instead, he was made to feel devalued. This led to developing a sense of entitlement as they held on to past resentments and cynicism. These kids were given the message their desires and needs did not matter, and in turn, this evolved into anger and bitterness.

As adults, when similar emotional pain erupts that causes the Inner Child to scream, *"My needs don't matter,"* the entitlement wheel starts in motion. And when this occurs, you probably experience a range of emotions that leave you resentful. I do not need to tell you that is a bad combination.

ANOTHER LABEL FOR THE ENTITLED-SPITEFUL CHILD COULD BE THE DEFIANT CHILD

When this Inner Child perceives things are going wrong (and they may not be), his attitude is to seek pleasure-enhancing activities. It does not matter if his actions are destructive because the mindset of *"I deserve this"* is more powerful than any sense of right and wrong. And that is where spitefulness can kick in and create chaos.

You should remember this unfortunate Child is hurting very much and that his emotional pain points have turned into anger.

THE INFERIOR-WEAK CHILD

As I mentioned before, I estimate 75% of the men I have worked with have been the victims of bullying. It cannot be emphasized enough the emotional suffering and the destruction caused by callous behavior. For many kids, being tormented by mean-spirited children and sometimes adults leads to low self-esteem and a self of worthlessness. In the worst case, it can result in suicide.

Over time, if this browbeating continues, some individuals will be conditioned to believe they are weak and inferior.

Again, this behavior can come at the hands of parents, siblings, peers, or other authority figures. The source does not matter; the outcome results in a child feeling subjacent to others, leading to severe consequences as an adult.

As they stumble upon sex, some adolescent boys use it to create newfound feelings of being empowered and forceful, while others utilize sex to reinforce their sense of inferiority.

THIS CHILD LIVES IN A DANGEROUS WORLD

"I was picked on at school and home," said Owen, who, although married, pays to role-play with domineering women. "There was no place I felt safe, and as I got older, I pictured myself weaker than other kids. As a teenager, I fantasized about mature women beating, humiliating, and telling me how unmanly I was. I have acted on those fantasies too many times as an adult."

Let us stop for a moment. Go back and re-read Owen's quote. This is where his Inner Child lives – in a dangerous world. He is a frightened Child who believes he is inferior to others. Therefore, this Inner Child is always on the lookout for what he perceives as situations that could make Owen feel weak.

When those situations arise, the Inner Child becomes activated, and his feelings of weakness send Owen into a world of submissive fantasy. If the emotions of feeling inferior become too intense, Owen will most likely need more stimulation than fantasy to escape the distress and will visit a dominatrix.

This Child can be one of the most troubling of the 12 children because of the damage he continues to inflict on these men and their partners.

"I am what you would call a 'dom' in the sex world," said Marvin, who lives a lifestyle that contradicts his role as a church deacon. "I seek out submissive men as sex partners. As a teenager, I started fantasizing about humiliating boys. I guess it had to do with the abuse I suffered at the hands of bullies. They tormented me. I would always be fearful of going to school. But when the fantasies started, although they didn't stop the bullying, at least I had a place I could run off to in my mind where I was the victor. For years, I have been the aggressor with numerous men. But I still feel fragile inside."

Like all 12 children, the Inferior-Weak Child temporarily overcomes his negative emotional pain points by utilizing harmful defense mechanisms. These are coping strategies developed at an early age to block the pain carried forth into your adult world.

THE STRESSED CHILD

Of the 12 reasons why men abuse sex, this is an immensely popular choice. The reason is straightforward – sex provides a chemical rush of euphoria that relaxes the body and mind

 and is a valuable tool for a stressed individual. Relaxation is accomplished by releasing various chemicals in the brain, including oxytocin, a potent hormone that is an antidote for depressive feelings. But let us take a step back. If you were one of these kids raised in a stressful and chaotic environment along the way, you probably learned several coping mechanisms (distractions) to block out most of your anxiety. However, utilizing these means of escape did not mean the tension was gone; it is just that you were able to avoid dwelling on it.

Even though you were raised in a chaotic environment, you probably appeared well-adjusted and happy as a child. But that is what others saw on the outside. What was beneath the iceberg was consistent worrying.

Over time, you learned to desensitize anxiousness to the point where you were basically oblivious to its existence. In fact, children sometimes are so good at keeping their anxiety hidden they do not realize its intensity. Some of my clients who describe themselves as carefree are some of the most anxious individuals I have ever met. They just did an excellent job of repressing it. Funny how the brain works.

But the truth of the matter is anxiety is never indeed entirely repressed. It leaks out. How? Here are some examples:

- Restlessness
- Awkwardness
- Obsessive-Compulsive Behaviors
- Isolating
- Over-reactivity
- Mood Swings
- Perfectionism
- Social Isolation
- Compulsiveness
- Addictive Behaviors
- Flat Affect
- Chronic Complaining of Physical Issues
- Defiant Behaviors
- Depression

Our Inner Child finds many ways to distract us from emotional anxiety, including imagination, food, television, Internet, sugar, reading, fantasizing, etc. But one of the most effective ways to sidetrack anxiety that we stumbled across was sex. With the rush of pleasure-enhancing chemicals, men use sex to get a satisfying and fulfilling rush that provides a carefree existence – even if only for a brief time.

As adults, they continue to utilize sex as a stress buster of choice. *"Visiting a massage parlor helps me unwind,"* said Gary, who is single and spends nearly $800 monthly at massage parlors. *"I realize it's not the right way to alleviate my stress, but it has the same effect that pornography did when I was a stressed-out teenager. It works."*

ONE OF THE MOST EFFECTIVE WAYS TO SIDETRACK ANXIETY IS SEX

Just as it did when you were a child, sex serves to soothe anxiety and take away the world's worries. That is until the orgasm is completed, and it is back to reality. Then anxiety can reappear, causing you to rely more heavily on sexual activities to lessen stress. You soon become caught in a vicious cycle that heightens your overall stress while adding a dose of shame to the equation.

Where to get your next fix, how to keep your secrets hidden, and the shamefulness of your activities all add to the stress level you initially sought to reduce. What started as a tension reliever has now become an addictive habit.

Serving as a stress buster should not be the function of sex. When we use sex the same way we use ibuprofen to relieve body aches, we diminish its real purpose: solidifying the emotional bond between a man and a woman. The adrenaline rush produced by pornography and other sexual activities should not be abused. And when we utilize sex to distract ourselves from stress, that is precisely what we do.

EARLY SEXUALLY STIMULATED/SEXUALLY ABUSED CHILD

When children endure sexual abuse, it changes everything. Their worldviews regarding people, security, trust, and innocence are dramatically altered. Various defense mechanisms are created to maintain a resemblance of sanity and safety.

Unfortunately, in many cases, these children hide their abuse. While statistics vary, studies show only 12 to 30 percent of child sex abuse cases, are reported. This means most children who suffer at the hands of sexual predators must learn how to cope alone with enormous shame and guilt. When a child carries the burden of harboring a horrible secret, it is a good bet he will suffer additional emotional and mental consequences along the way.

Others in this group were subjected to sexual stimulation far too early. This early exposure may have been accidentally stumbling across pornography or environmental exposure to sex. For example, one of my clients would hear his parents having sex several nights a week through the walls of their adjoining bedrooms.

"I would lay in bed listening to the sounds coming from their bedroom," recalled Bruce, who was court-mandated to attend counseling after being arrested for putting video-

recording equipment in the women's restroom at work. *"I had no idea what was*

going on, but over time, I found it more and more thrilling. I can remember the moaning coming from their room. This went on for years, and as a teenager, I would masturbate to their sounds."

This environmental exposure made him a full-blown voyeur who would take photos looking under the skirts of unsuspecting women.

Early sexual stimulation can lead to many irrational beliefs about sex and the individual himself, including the impression he is "dirty" and people are "objects." In that case, the Inner Child may call on us to use sex to punish ourselves or hurt others.

Obsessive thoughts about sex and chronic masturbation can also be an outcome faced by adults who fall into this category. This obsessive thinking results from the brain becoming hard-wired to crave the chemical rush that comes from repeated sexual exposure, therefore requiring men to turn to sex repeatedly for a quick kick.

"I found myself looking at porn and masturbating an average of 5-6 times a day," said Larry, who lost several jobs due to watching pornography at work. "I was molested by a babysitter for nearly five years, starting when I was six. She also introduced me to pornography. Even after the molestation stopped, I couldn't stop thinking about sex. I would watch porn on the Internet whenever I could. It just gave me an amazing emotional feeling. I felt excited and yet calm."

As I said earlier, when a child endures sexual abuse, it changes everything.

HEADS UP: If this is your story and you have not sought professional help, I ask that you please consider doing so. Healing from these horrific childhood wounds is possible.

THE ENMESHED CHILD

These children struggled to form their identities and often were conditioned to care for others at the expense of their emotions and needs. Others were consistently pampered and believed they were entitled to special treatment, which led them to become overly dependent on their parent(s) and later, as adults, on others.

The Enmeshed Child is overly complex to understand because enmeshment can take on many different forms and lead to numerous outcomes – none that are healthy. Enmeshment can involve one or both parents and sometimes work its way throughout the entire family.

Whether a parent demands a child's attention or smothers the child, the same premise is at work – a lack of relational boundaries.

Parents of these children place unreasonable burdens on the shoulders of their kids. They may use a child as a surrogate spouse or require family secrets to be kept from the outside world. A child's life is not his own but is dictated by the desires of the enmeshed parent(s).

ENMESHMENT CAN TAKE ON MANY DIFFERENT FORMS AND LEAD TO NUMEROUS OUTCOMES – NONE ARE HEALTHY

Other children deal with parents who are overly involved in their lives. There is little if any privacy as parents micromanage the child. In all enmeshment scenarios, children feel enormous levels of anxiousness, whether attempting to identify and cater to the parents' needs or trying to slip away from the parents' overbearing grips.

Parents who exert control over their children's day-to-day activities normally do not stop as children reach adulthood.

There may be a continuous conflict if an adult child tries to break free of the parents' strongholds – including mental or emotional abuse, manipulation, and guilt from other family members.

Parents may not only seek emotional support for their children but also expect them not to move away, marry a spouse they approve of, and pursue certain career paths. It is common for enmeshed children to feel trapped in their lifestyles and controlled and manipulated by their parents. They also may struggle to establish healthy relationships or possess strong self-worth.

THE SPIRITUALLY WOUNDED CHILD

Spiritually Wounded Children can find themselves emotionally crippled for life due to the damage they experience at the hands of individuals who claim to be spiritual mentors or leaders.

These children may have little faith or hope in themselves and lack confidence in others to be dependable, trustworthy, and honest. A child can become spiritually wounded at home or in an institutional setting.

Forced to live by rigid religious standards or having their lives scripted by others, these children fear making mistakes and disappointing others.

"My parents were always preaching scripture in our home," said Avery, a 48-year-old married man with two adult children. Avery came to counseling after attending a two-week residential program to start his recovery from pornography. *"Any thoughts or behaviors my sister and I had were scrutinized by our parents using the Bible. Anything we did was never good enough, and we second-guessed every action we considered.*

"Our home felt so restrictive and uneasy," he continued. "When I found porn around 13, it served as a wonderful distraction. My sister discovered sex with boys and became pregnant at 16. She rebelled hard against my parents."

Spiritually Wounded Children are extremely anxious and struggle to meet the requirements asked of them. Shame and fear were tools individuals used to exert control and mandate religious rules and obligations to push righteous behaviors. Children often felt they could not maintain these standards, so they dealt with tremendous guilt. The Spiritually Wounded Child feels unsafe.

THE UNWANTED CHILD

Imagine you did not belong anywhere or to anyone. Ponder the prospect of doing ANYTHING to fit in and feel that you

mattered. That is often the case with Unwanted Children. These emotionally torn individuals received the message directly or indirectly that they were a burden to their caregivers. And if given a choice to do things over again, these caregivers would have elected not to have these children.

Here are a few of the many reasons why a mother may struggle to bond with her child.

- The child is one of many, and the mother is overwhelmed
- The mother was herself unwanted
- The mother is young and not ready for the responsibility
- The mother was raped or perhaps hated the child's father
- The mother feels having the child has trapped her into staying in an unhappy relationship

This lack of emotional attachment may leave children feeling rejected and unloved. As adults, they possess attachment wounds that impede their relationships and ability to nurture healthy emotional relationships with others. Many deal with an anxious-avoidant attachment style in which they may desire to engage with others but struggle to connect. Their relationships stay at a 10,000-foot level; therefore, they do not need to depend upon anyone.

Others develop an anxious-preoccupied attachment style, which worries them about whether their relationship needs will be met. And while there is a desire to be in a healthy relationship, there also may be a fear of abandonment and rejection, making it difficult to trust people.

Some Unwanted Children were adopted. Even if raised in a loving and accepting home, some children felt they did not belong. They struggle to overcome knowing their natural parents gave them away.

"I don't know the circumstances why my parents put me up for adoption," said Raul, who acknowledges his adoptive parents were amazing people. "All I know is I could never give a child up for adoption, no matter the circumstances. They could have made it work, but they elected to toss me aside."

PROBLEMATIC SEXUAL BEHAVIORS CREATE RUNNERS

So, there you have it — the 12 Inner Children who impact a man's PSBs. Perhaps you noticed each of these children represents a unique emotional wound that, over time, manifested like cancer in their souls.

These Inner Children bring a psychological complexity not understood by those who struggle with PSBs or their partners. But once individuals recognize their Inner Children are running the show, they are prepared to go on a journey of recovery that goes far beyond behavioral modification. They are placed on a pathway that will change their hearts and lead them to become men of integrity.

"When we first started talking about the Inner Child in therapy, I was confused," recalls Ralph, whose PSBs involved prostitutes, affairs, and pornography. "But as we continued to explore, and I kept digging deeper and deeper into the causes of my behavior, I found the entire process exciting. You get a sense of freedom and empowerment when you realize why you do the things you do. It has been eye-opening and enriching for me."

One common theme runs throughout these 12 rationales — all need stimulating distractions to divert from the emotional discomfort. In many cases, the distress results from events that occurred years or decades ago and have been locked away in our subconscious minds. Unaware of what we genuinely feel during anxious moments leave us frustrated as we try to determine why we engage in sexual behaviors that are destructive to ourselves and others.

The truth is we do not recognize the core emotional triggers that lead us to act out sexually because we refuse to sit with the pain they cause. However, our Inner Child is very much in tune with them. That is why it is critical to connect deeper with the Child and understand the troubling emotions that activate him.

With proper professional help, a man can identify the core emotional triggers that cause his Inner Child to have tantrums and push him to escape toward toxic sexual behaviors. When men get their hands dirty and touch raw nerves that activate their Inner Child, they discover their emotional pain is more profound and intense than they ever imagined. But with insights into what triggers the child comes the ability to develop an action plan to instruct and comfort him. In doing so, men who struggle with PSBs can better manage their unwanted behaviors.

"When I first went into counseling for my pornography addiction, I simply thought it was a bad habit I developed as a teenager," said Bobby, who tried multiple times with little success to stop his pornography habit. "But I understood my

Inner Child saw pornography as a resource to reduce the anxiety I experienced as a child living with alcoholic parents.

"The stress I experienced led me to become a perfectionist and a work-alcoholic," he continued. "At work, when I felt I wasn't in control of things, it activated my Inner Child, who was taken back to times when chaos ruled my home. So, he pushed me to run away from dealing with my feelings of being powerless and instead turn to pornography and masturbation."

Men like Bobby have Inner Children who are "runners." They struggle to confront the emotional demons they experienced in their youth and instead seek to ignore them by utilizing sex. By running, they do not need to face negative emotions. Instead, they keep distancing themselves from the potential pain by engaging in sexual activities that stimulate and distract.

Unfortunately, there is a high price to pay for their inability to confront the feelings that haunt them. By not knowing how to deal with their emotional brokenness, they suffer consequences such as broken relationships, financial hardships, loss of employment, sexually transmitted diseases, and legal difficulties, to name a few. It is a sad situation that leaves many men feeling shameful and hopeless.

WHY BOTHER?

You are probably asking yourself, *"Why should understanding the reason(s) I abuse sex be part of my recovery."* Good question. The answer is the reason(s) allow you to get to the root of your destructive sexual behavior. Without understanding why you use sex to distract from your underlying emotional discomfort, you limit your ability to get to the bedrock of the problem. Defeating PSBs should not be limited to changing behaviors but should involve changing a man's heart.

In working with hundreds of men who struggle with PSBs, I have found that those who succeed are on a journey of self-reflection and a continuous search for insight into themselves and their PSBs. They want answers to the question, *"Why do I think, feel, and behave the way I do?"*

They are on a quest to finish strong as men and rebuild their legacies. The conquerors of PSBs regularly analyze their current emotional, mental, physical, and spiritual states. Rather than be reactive, they learn to become mindful and responsive in trying circumstances, which helps them realize when their Inner Children are activated.

They learn to stay one step ahead of the Child to avoid wandering aimlessly down the rabbit hole, leading to sexual turmoil.

A key in this transformation process is understanding **why** you turned to sex as a distraction in the first place. And to accomplish that, you must become aware and involved with your Inner Child.

EXTREMELY IMPORTANT INFORMATION

Let us stop here to once again reinforce the point that these 12 reasons are NOT excuses for men's inappropriate use of sex. They should serve as insights to help men identify and deal with hidden emotional pain, they medicate by using sex as a distraction and/or stimulant. Men should in no way hide behind these rationales as justification for their poor behaviors. Instead, these reasons should be utilized as tools in the recovery process to help provide much needed self-reflection about why they engage in destructive behaviors. Always "own" your stuff.

GETTING STARTED

As we continue, I will ask you to challenge yourself in ways you have never been before. We will go beyond your PSBs and explore the emotional pain and scars people and events left upon you as a child and/or teenager. We will drill deep to uncover the core of your PSBs and discover your Inner Child's core emotional triggers.

I will be honest with you. This process can be extremely painful, but in the end, you will experience a sense of relief and freedom you have never felt. You will have the insights needed to assist you against temptation and to help you comfort your Inner Child and effectively manage your PSBs.

Moving forward, we will review the 12 children more in-depth, and with careful analysis, you will uncover the children you believe drive you toward unhealthy sexual behaviors. It is rare to select only one child, and most men resonate with four to six that thoroughly explain their obsession with sex. Some clients have chosen all 12.

After carefully reviewing the list, prioritize them based on which ones you associate with most. Based on the introduction for each child you just finished reading, you probably have already started to draw conclusions about those children that relate to your PSBs. But be patient with this process. As you review each child more in-depth, you will develop greater self-awareness and insights that may change or add to your initial selections.

The key is to reflect on each of these children and not rush through the process. You want to walk away with clarity, enabling you to create an effective game plan to manage your PSBs moving forward. So, let us begin this new and exciting journey.

Before moving on, now that you have a snapshot of the 12 Inner Children who comprise the Inner Child Model™, which ones do you believe you identify with most? You probably have some idea, but do not be surprised if your selections change as you move forward and develop a deeper understanding of each child. Be sure as you move ahead to use your workbook or a journal to track the Inner Children you select, as well as the Core Emotional Triggers associated with each.

CHAPTER 4

Reason 1: The Bored Child

"The two enemies of human happiness are pain and boredom."
—Arthur Schopenhauer, Philosopher

For Peter, being a porn addict is hell. The 36-year-old auto mechanic has been married for 12 years with two children and claims he cannot remember when he did not watch porn. And as you can imagine, bringing a porn problem into his marriage has been a source of significant tension between him and his wife.

"The bottom line is, I need it, and she hates it," he said during one of our counseling sessions as he began the usual justification argument for his problem. "We always fight about it because I cannot give it up. I mean, I would like to, but I cannot do it. I have tried hundreds of times, but I just ended up failing. I wish she would accept it for what it is and leave me alone.

"I have a tough time understanding what she's so upset about," he continued. "It's not like I'm having sex with other women. I'm watching other women have sex."

As a child, Peter grew up surrounded by five people – his parents and three older brothers. He surprised his parents, who thought they were done having children. His youngest brother was six years older than him when Peter came along. His older brothers were 12 and 10, which created a significant age gap between the siblings.

"By the time I was walking and talking, none of my brothers wanted to have anything to do with me," Peter recalls. "My two oldest brothers were a handful, getting in trouble at school and with the law, which required much of my parents' time. As a kid, I always played alone. The more I think about it, I always felt bored growing up."

At eight, Peter came across a stack of an older brother's Hustler magazines. "After looking at a few pages, I was hooked," he recalled. "Whenever I got the chance, I would steal one from his room and spend hours lost viewing it. I believe it may have been the first time in my life that I ever felt excited about something."

BORED OF BEING BORED BECAUSE BEING BORED IS "BORING"

Can you imagine looking back and recalling the first time you felt mentally and emotionally excited came at the hands of activity as dark as pornography? If you ask most people to recall their most exciting childhood memory, you might get answers such as a pony ride, a birthday party, a new puppy, or a trip to Disney World. But pornography? How does that become a man's earliest memory of being mentally and emotionally stimulated?

Because prior to the first glance at porn, these young boys' lives lack stimulation. When Peter described pornography's ability to make him feel "excited," he recalled an early moment when he felt an enormous rush of stimulation. The sexual images he saw produced an invigoration he had never experienced in his quiet and isolated world. It was an electrifying experience that opened and engaged neuropathways that generated curiosity and wonderment. And it is something his Inner Child never forgot.

For boys like Peter, stimulating interaction with others was limited or non-existent, leaving them to rely on their imaginations to generate excitement. After a while, that becomes tiresome, and boredom reappears.

Some boys begin to employ their first addictive behavior to escape boredom as they become glued to the television, the Internet, video games, or overeat. These activities help distract from the mental and emotional distress of feeling bored and isolated. However, these endeavors cannot replace healthy, interactive relationships, which we all desire, whether consciously or subconsciously. And over time, these forms of entertainment may become tiring.

"I remember thinking to myself when I was a kid that television was my friend," chuckled Lucas, whose parents were alcoholics. "It wasn't unusual for me to go several days without seeing either of my parents. They would go off partying and stay away for days. So, I had to fend for myself, and television became my buddy. I want to say it kept me from being bored, but it didn't. I was still bored until I discovered pornography. Then things were rarely boring."

The Inner Child of men who grew up with little stimulation is emotionally triggered today when events leave them feeling rejected, abandoned, lonely, fearful, or bored, to name a few.

How It Went Wrong

As you will see, there are numerous reasons why a child grows up in an empty or low-key environment that provides little positive stimulation. One is parents who ignore the emotional needs of their children. These parents spent too much time focusing on their issues and desires instead of looking outward and focusing on their sons. They assumed if a child was not complaining, everything was okay, and the kid was happy. But those parents could not have been more wrong.

"My dad left us when I was an infant," recalls Stan, who battles with pornography. "It was just Mom and me. But really, it was just me. Starting in first grade, when I got home, I would be alone until 7 pm, when she finally got home. And then she would be so tired she would crash in front of the television or go into her bedroom. It would be a lot if she spent 10 minutes with me at night. But I wasn't going to complain. She would not have liked that.

"At age seven, I was cooking my meals, getting myself ready for school, and washing clothes," he recalled. "Truthfully, I didn't even mind the chores or caring for myself. It was coming home to an empty apartment that troubled me the most. I knew I would be bored and lonely once I walked through the door. It felt like a 10-ton boulder around my neck. It sucked."

Although Stan was raised by a single mom, he was rearing himself. His mother was overwhelmed with being the sole provider and did not have the energy to provide him with attention and nurturing. Placing a child in a role where they must learn to survive on their own teaches them to be "ultra" independent, which is unhealthy.

THE DISTRACTED PARENT

As adults, these men tend to have difficulty asking others for help. And for a man trying to recover from PSBs, this is a real problem. The lone wolf nearly always fails when it comes to recovery. Studies have demonstrated having a support network and sponsor dramatically increases the likelihood of successful recovery. But when you do not know how to ask for help or refuse to ask, you put yourself and your recovery at a disadvantage.

Others were raised in families where a sibling suffered from a mental, emotional, or physical disability that demanded much of their parents' time and attention. It is difficult to ask for attention from a parent overwhelmed by caring for an ill brother or sister.

"I was one of two kids in my family," said Lawrence, whose marriage ended because of the debt he incurred with prostitutes and at strip clubs. "My sister was born with Spina Bifida. Her illness took up much of my parents' time and caused a lot of stress between them. It was not a happy home, so I would spend a lot of time in my room. I can remember the pain I felt that I didn't really matter. It created an incredible sadness in me that I still experience today."

Children raised in a home with a significant age difference among their siblings may also find themselves experiencing overwhelming periods of loneliness and boredom.

"I was the youngest of nine children," recalls Ty, who has battled with pornography since seeing it in middle school. "But my closest sibling was six years older than me, and she never paid attention to me. By the time I was five, only my sister and I were left at home. The rest of my brothers and sisters had moved out. Oh, and it's probably important for you to know my father died when I was four.

IT IS NOT UNUSUAL FOR THESE CHILDREN TO ESCAPE THEIR LOW-KEY REALITY BY ENGAGING IN FANTASIES THAT ARE NOT SEXUAL

"Mom was so focused on working the farm, and my sister took care of the house," he continued. "I had no one to play with. I can remember feeling bored and lonely often. That is until a kid at school showed me some stag magazines. Now that was interesting, and it seemed that whenever I had access to pornography, life became entertaining."

Isolation and boredom are the norms for those raised in an environment that offers little positive interaction among family members. Even if people surrounded them, these young boys felt isolated and alone due to the lack of personal engagement they experienced. They were left unchallenged to grow and develop mentally, emotionally, and spiritually.

Instead, these kids grew up learning to entertain themselves and spent much time in fantasy and daydreaming. They developed the unhealthy habit of "staying in their heads."

"I always wondered what was wrong with me," said Carl, who, at 49, has dealt with PSBs for nearly three decades. "In my entire life, I have never had any real passions. There have been moments of happiness here and here, but I feel as though I am simply walking through life most of the time. My relationships lack passion. My work lacks passion. There is no passion, period. While I don't want to kill myself, I wouldn't be sad if it was my time to go."

Although he does not consider it, sex has been Carl's passion. It is a driving force in his world, and he turns to it several times a day to stimulate what he perceives as a mundane life.

"Whenever I am bored – which is too frequently – I start searching the escort ads," said Carl. "I always tell myself I am just going to look, but it never ends there, and I end up acting out. When I go through the ads, it's like I am hunting, and that's sometimes more exciting than the sexual experience itself."

A life lacking stimulation causes Carl to seek continuous mental and emotional jump-starts. He uses sex to create sparks he knows will generate an emotional inferno of bliss that cannot be achieved by any other means. Sexual stimulation —real or merely fantasy — is the antidote to pushing aside boredom and lack of purpose that has haunted him all his life.

PORN AND SEX: THE ULTIMATE STIMULATORS

As you can imagine, this empty, quiet existence experienced by children and teenagers brings little in the way of stimulating beyond the child's imagination. That is, until they stumble across sex and experience a heightened level of stimulation, unlike anything they had ever felt.

"I remember I was around 14 years old when I came across a collection of VHS porn tapes my father hid in the back of his closet," said Charlie, who had more than a dozen physical and emotional affairs during his nine-year marriage. "I must admit, at first, I didn't know what I was looking at, but I knew I liked it. As I watched, I experienced an intoxication of excitement I had never felt before. What was strange is the frenzy I experienced wasn't just sexual, it was also emotional.

"On that day, something changed in me, and whenever my parents left me alone – which was often – I would dig through the closet and pull out the videos. I didn't know it then, but I was getting buzzed. It was like you dropped me in the middle of a candy store and said, 'Go at it.' I couldn't stop. I was feeling something for the first time."

The feelings Charlie felt with pornography were overpowering and captivated him like nothing he had ever experienced. For men who grow up in low-stimulation environments, the discovery of sex is an internal waking. Their attention is laser-focused on sex as they feed their newfound desire for stimulation. They feel alive, and life has finally provided something to look forward to. Sex serves as the mental and emotional rush that creates surreal experiences.

IT IS NOT UNCOMMON FOR THESE MEN TO BECOME ADRENALINE JUNKIES

But with this new excitement comes the changing of a young man's heart – innocence is lost. They start to look at girls differently.

"I was 13 when I happened upon pornography online," said Chris, a senior in college who had been dealing with a pornography addiction that led him to masturbate up to five times daily. *"Before that time, I never paid much attention to the girls I would hang with at school. But after seeing porn, I could not help but look at them differently. And to make matters worse, I wanted to touch them. I remember roughhousing with some of them so I could 'innocently' touch various parts of their bodies."*

When a young boy's first encounter with sex is pornography, he obtains a flawed view of sex. He learns to objectify women and sees them as a source of self-gratification. Sex is perceived as nothing more than a physical act with the end objective of achieving an orgasm. And others are nothing more than vehicles to accomplish this selfish goal. This may not mean these boys do not like or love their partners, but that is secondary to physical intimacy.

This inability to see people as more than mere toys is an unrealistic means of justifying our struggle with lust. Now, we add boredom to the lust equation and develop out-of-control sexual cravings that lead us to seek stimulation by abusing sex. This confusion puts us on a path toward behaviors that can be destructive to ourselves and others.

"I thought sex was about a woman giving herself to a man for his pleasure," Chris continued. "At least that is the message pornography gives you. When I dated, I didn't see a woman; I saw a plaything. She was supposed to be at my call when I wanted sex. And when it didn't work out that way, I would become upset and sulk. It's no wonder I couldn't keep a girlfriend."

NOT MORE – DIFFERENT

The Bored Child is content with life for brief periods, but it never lasts long. A new video game loses its excitement faster for the Bored Child than other kids. Even the taste of food can become routine with each serving.

The Bored Child is on a continuous quest to discover new activities that quiet his sense of boredom. He finds himself running from activity to activity to fill an empty void. Even porn and sex can become routine, and this is where escalation comes into play for this individual.

"I can recall when looking at a naked woman would arouse me," said Steward, who is trying to patch together his 28-year marriage after he was discovered by his wife downloading masochistic pornography. *"I never imagined one day I would look at photos of women being tortured and humiliated and be aroused. But after years of watching porn, none of it was stimulating. When I came across this genre, it was extremely different. It also was extremely intense."*

While it is common for men to escalate into different genres of porn, that alone may not be enough for some men.

"Massage parlors, escorts, strip clubs, adult bookstores, and transexuals," said Milton when asked about the problematic sexual behaviors he engaged in. "I think I have done everything, although I am not sure that is an accurate statement. But it sure feels like I have.

"Although I never stopped watching porn, it didn't provide the same rush it once did," he continued. "I was tired of spending hours looking for a certain video that would provide the rush I needed. When I had sex with others, the stimulation was always present."

LYLE'S STORY

Lyle is a recent college graduate about to become engaged to his high-school sweetheart, Karen. However, Lyle has a secret he has been hiding from his future bride. He likes to visit massage parlors.

I do not need to explain that massage parlors and marriages struggle to co-exist in an overwhelming percentage of cases.

Fortunately, Lyle wanted to change and sought counseling to determine why he struggled with lust.

"I have always felt guilty about going to those places, just like when I watch porn," he said. "But now that I am getting married, I must get this out of my life. I hate that I have been unfaithful to Karen already, and I want to be a good husband. She deserves that from me."

Lyle grew up in a loving home with his parents and an older sister. "Life was good," he recalled. "Mom and Dad were around, attending all of my sporting events. I got along with my sister. There was little in the way of arguing or conflict in our house."

As we continued to explore Lyle's family of origin, we discovered that while there was little conflict, there was little in the way of engagement and stimulation. It was not unusual for the family to have dinner in front of the television. It was common for them to retreat to their places in the house after eating — Dad in the den watching TV, Mom in her sewing and craft room, his sister in her bedroom, and Lyle in his bedroom. They were four people living under one roof but strangers.

Spending a great deal of time isolated from his family, Lyle discovered pornography and sexually charged chatrooms. He found it all to be very thrilling. And unlike video games, which would become monotonous over time, sex never lost its luster.

"It's amazing to discover I use sex to keep feelings of boredom away," Lyle said. "You would think a guy starting a career and about to get engaged would never feel bored. But I feel that way often. Even Karen says I lack passion, and it's difficult for me to get excited about anything. And she's right.

"I remember as a teenager, the only thing I truly got excited about was sex. Even though I was highly active in sports like football and basketball, nothing had the allure of sex," he continued. "And the more I acted out, the more I wanted. When I discovered massage parlors around 17, I would save every dollar I earned with my part-time job to spend it there. Because it was taboo, it was exciting. Now, it all seems like such a waste."

WHEN MEN CHEAPEN SEX, THEY LIMIT THEIR ABILITY TO GENERATE HEALTHY AND AUTHENTIC RELATIONSHIPS

Lyle put his trust in sex to keep him from being bored, and sex ended up a straitjacket. Sex should not be the outlet to solve a man's emotional turmoil and distress. We need to learn how to take hold of our psychological afflictions and manage them. It is time to stop running away from discomfort and utilizing sex as a source of temporary relief. Sex is a gift God gives us to procreate and solidify intimacy between a man and a woman.

When men cheapen sex, they limit their ability to generate healthy and authentic relationships. Sex, when performed alone or with individuals in an emotionally detached way, is simply a physical act. And over time, it can produce feelings of discontent and shame. That is why men who abuse sex desperately seek to hide their actions in the dark. They fear others knowing their secrets because their actions are rooted in shame.

"As an elder in my church, I would die if someone found out about my sexual sins," said David. "I go to great lengths to hide my actions. It's incredible how much time I spend covering my tracks. But I hate it. I hate all of it: the acting out and the deceit. It leaves sex feeling so ugly and dirty.

"But I can't help myself," he continued. "It is the only thing that makes me feel alive. Ever since I was a young child, I felt dead inside. I grew up very lonely and extremely bored. And even though I am married, I feel the same way today. I'm dead inside. I need those encounters at adult bookstores and strip clubs to feel something. Even though I end up hating how I feel after it's over."

That is what living in a world that lacked stimulation as a child can do to an adult. David had been conditioned at an early age when he saw pornography to equate sex as the go-to source of stimulation to distract from his feelings of boredom. However, this abuse of sex, in the end, leaves men feeling the same way they did as children – empty.

Although porn or sexual activities may have helped bored boys kill time – as adults – many realize porn is a waste of time.

"I have come to realize through therapy that pornography has been nothing more than my escape from a life that lacked stimulation," said Ben, who, as he got older, shifted from pornography to risky sexual activities, including soliciting street prostitutes. "Looking back, I can see how viewing porn provided a rush I could not achieve in other areas of my life. But it saddens me when I realize the limited thrills I achieved came from exploiting others."

KID TALK

Along with helping your Inner Child process painful emotional triggers, how else can you comfort this Child? Start by educating him that boredom is a choice. By adjusting our mindset, we can seek creative and healthy ways to keep our minds active.

This child must be encouraged to explore life and take risks by seeking new, healthy experiences. The Bored Child desires to participate in exciting activities that provide positive stimulation. What these activities are will depend upon your interests. Now I hear you saying, *"But I don't have any interests."* Perhaps. But that becomes part of your journey — seeking out potential activities to generate newfound passions.

Stuck for ideas? I tell my clients, *"Google is your friend."* Use it to generate ideas that can bring positive excitement into your life. For example, by Googling *"What Bored Adults Can Do,"* you will find numerous articles such as *"96 Things to Do When You're Bored."* Again, it is about becoming curious and exploring potential activities to overcome boredom.

CORE EMOTIONAL TRIGGERS

The chart below provides a list of core emotional triggers that can activate the Inner Child who grew up bored and isolated. If boredom is one of your reasons **why**, select one or more of these core emotional triggers that sting when you think about them. Start keeping a list of the triggers you select throughout the book. These will help you identify when your Inner Child is triggered.

Why are core emotional triggers so important? Because you act out when your Inner Child is activated, and he becomes activated when one of your core emotional triggers kicks in.

If you realize he is triggered, you can work to quiet him by ensuring him that you are in charge of the situation and can handle it. He wants to know if an adult is available to deal with the emotional discomfort.

Core Emotional Triggers of the Bored Inner Child

This is only a partial list, and you may identify additional triggers. Remember, his emotions occur based on the way he perceives a current situation. However, his perception of evens may be inccurate.

Life is boring	I am alone
I am invisible	I feel empty
I do not measure up	I feel restless
Life has no purpose	

What Core Emotional Triggers did you select?

TAKE A MOMENT: If you resonate with the Bored Child, describe growing up at home, school, and with friends. Can you recall your first strong adrenaline rush? Explain that experience. Try to get in touch and talk with your Inner Child. Do not be discouraged if you are not successful immediately.

EXTREMELY IMPORTANT
INFORMATION

We just reviewed scenarios of home environments that lacked stimulation. Please note, this is not a complete list of examples. As you ponder your childhood you may find you experienced different circumstances that led to a low-key existence. That is ok. Space does not permit me to cover every potential negative scenario that could impact us as children.

And there are no cookie-cutter answers to determining what led to your PSBs. And that is true for each of the 12 children outlined in this book.

Challenge yourself to explore deeper what you experienced in your youth and the impact it had on your Inner Child. The more you explore and self-reflect, the more conclusive your answer to the **why** question will become.

CHAPTER 5

Reason 2: The Unnoticed Child

"The only thing worse than parents who don't pay attention to you is parents who pat you on the shoulder on their way out the door."

— Katie Alender, Author

When he walked into my office, I could tell Sean was a very reserved and quiet man. He shuffled when he walked, and he made limited eye contact. I soon discovered this 51-year-old married man had five affairs and numerous one-night stands. Two weeks ago, his wife of 23 years found out about his troubling ventures and demanded he seek therapy.

"I'm not going to lie. If it weren't for the fact my marriage was at stake, I probably wouldn't be there," Sean said, his eyes shifting everywhere except in my direction. I tried recalling when I last saw a man who exhibited such anxiety. *"You need to know I love my wife. But I enjoy time with different women. It makes me feel special when they take an interest in me."*

Sean lowered his head after making that comment, and immediately, I suspected he had struggled his entire life to achieve a sense of belonging. As he started to tell his story, my beliefs were confirmed.

As a child, Sean grew up in the inner city with a single mother. Their neighborhood was dangerous, and he was not allowed outdoors unless escorted by his mom, a rule that remained in place until he went to college.

As you can imagine, school was anxious for a kid like Sean, who was meek and endured bullying and isolation. Over the years, it became difficult to make friends, so he stopped trying. Instead, he focused on studying and spent much of his time in the school library.

At home, it was more isolation. His mother worked long hours, and when she did get home, it brought no joy to Sean's heart. His mother was cold and distant. Longing for attention, he did not receive at school, instead, he received frigid responses from a woman who gave him the indirect message, *"You're not worth my time. I don't want you around unless I call you."* Although she never uttered those words, her actions and inactions repeatedly gave this impression to a small boy whose spirit was crushed. And it is that message his Inner Child still holds onto tightly and believes today.

SOME PEOPLE SHOULD CHANGE THEIR FACEBOOK STATUS TO "NEED ATTENTION"

"I may be exaggerating, but I truly can't remember one time when my mother sought me out to spend time with me," he recalled, looking like he was drifting off into space. "Even if I hurt myself, she would not go out of her way to help me. And now, as an adult, she still acts as though I am invisible when I'm around her."

So how does Sean's stone-like emotional mother correlate with his need to engage in sex with multiple women despite being "happily" married? The women provided the attention and interest he craved as a youngster. It did not matter their appearance or age; he was drawn to their desire to spend time with him.

"They make me feel wanted," he said during one of our early sessions. "And that emotion for me is like a drug. It gives me such a rush that I can't get enough. I dreamed of experiencing it growing up, but it never happened."

Now, you may be asking yourself, what about his wife? Does she not show him attention? Like others who suffered emotional abuse and/or neglect as a child, Sean married a woman like his mother. She was the only woman he ever dated, and although he describes her as sweet, she is not touchy-feely. Sean says she will "never" chase him or actively express a desire to be with him. Therefore, he experiences the same emotional depletion from his wife as he did as a child.

"I knew my wife was not the type of woman I wanted to be with, but she was the first and only person who ever paid any attention to me," he said, pointing out they met during his junior year in college. "And I think she saw me as a safe choice – a guy who is socially awkward and quiet. She probably felt I wouldn't need much from her because she had little to offer regarding love and affection.

CHILDHOOD EMOTIONAL NEGLECT

Sean is one of those men who endured Childhood Emotional Neglect (CEN). According to Dr. Jonice Webb, the author of *Running on Empty*, CEN results from parents failing to respond to a child's emotional needs. When this occurs, a child turns to the defense mechanism of tuning out many emotions.

"Growing up in a household that is either blind to your emotions or intolerant to what you feel requires a child to adapt to their situation," Dr. Webb says. "To ensure you do not burden your parents with your feelings or emotional needs, you push your emotions down and away. You become intolerant of your feelings, and you try hard to have no needs."

Pushing aside his emotions is what Sean did as a child to protect himself from feeling sad and lonely when no one was paying attention to him.

"I remember telling myself around the age of 9 that I did not need anyone," he recalled. "And I did an excellent job of convincing myself of that. Even when I did marry my wife, I knew she wasn't madly in love with me. But it was okay because I didn't really need anything from her.

"Shortly after we married, I started getting depressed," Sean continued. "My wife was distant, and now, after doing my recovery work, I understand it reminded me of life with mom. I was lonely but didn't want to admit it. That's when I started having affairs and one-night stands. And unbelievably, it would lift my depression. I now realize I was seeking attention from these women, not sex. In fact, often, I didn't even have sex with them. We would hang out, and that's enough for me."

WHY IS ATTENTION IMPORTANT?

Who does not like attention? As a kid, the thought of grandma reaching out to hug us and pinching our cheeks was warming, especially if she had a $10 bill in her hand. Attention is part of the human need to belong. It soothes the soul to know others who long to spend time with you.

CHILDHOOD EMOTIONAL NEGLECT LEADS CHILDREN TO IGNORE EMOTIONS; IT IS THE SAME WITH MEN STRUGGLING WITH PSBS

But being popular and in demand was something other people experienced – not you. And with that came the belief people were not interested. Not being pursued, you sat on the sidelines, waiting for someone to look your way. But it rarely or never happened.

Growing up, young boys like Sean never felt they belonged. They were outcasted and had to chase friends and family members. But rarely did they catch anyone.

In an article in Psychology Today magazine, Dr. Robert Mauer points out that when an individual struggles to feel desired as a child, the pain never entirely disappears.

"We take for granted that children require attention," he writes. "Many weary parents come home at night, digging deep inside to find the energy they aren't sure they have to give their little ones the affection they require. But what happens to this need as we grow and become adults? The answer: Nothing changes. The basic human need for attention remains, although sadly, most adults ignore this in both themselves and others."

SEAN'S INNER CHILD

Go back to a word Sean used in an earlier quote. He said his mother made him feel "invisible." Invisible is an essential word regarding Sean's PSBs because when his Inner Child feels "invisible," Sean is at higher risk of acting out inappropriately with women.

IT SOOTHES THE SOUL TO KNOW OTHERS LONG TO SPEND TIME WITH YOU

"There is a chill that goes through my body whenever someone doesn't acknowledge me," he said as he outlined several places where this could occur, including at work and church. "I remember my mother coming home and not saying anything to me. It was like she didn't know I was there, but I was right in front of her. I felt invisible, and it was frightening."

Loneliness is also among several core emotional triggers that can activate Sean's Inner Child. Here is a list of other triggers he identified in his recovery work. Please note while many of these emotions seem similar, they could feel quite different based on the circumstances he encounters.

- I feel abandoned
- I have been dismissed
- I do not belong
- I feel empty
- I am forgotten

"It's funny, but when you have been as lonely as I have throughout my life, many times you don't even recognize it's something you're experiencing at the moment," he explained. "It becomes natural. And you accept people are not going to pay attention to you."

While this experience may feel natural for Sean, it is completely uncomfortable for his inner kid. As I explained earlier, Little Sean is trapped in a time warp, and he vividly remembers the hurt and pain caused by the rejection he suffered at the hands of his mom and others.

So, while Sean may think he has learned to tune out his negative thinking, his little guy will help remind him by using many different techniques, including sexual imagery, objectifying women, and lustful fantasies. Let us examine an example of how core negative emotions impact Sean's world.

THE INNER CHILD RUNNING THE SHOW

Hoping to bridge the relationship with his mom, Sean invites her to his home for Christmas. She agrees to show up on Christmas Eve and spend three days. However, before anyone was up early on Christmas morning, she leaves the house and does not return.

When Sean and his family discover his mom has skipped out on them, his wife is livid. She starts expressing how selfish his mother is to sneak out in the early morning, not even exchanging gifts with her grandchildren.

Instead of dealing with his feelings of betrayal that his mom had yet again rejected him, he gets angry with her for the hurt and disappointment she caused his family. He dives right into defending his wife, saying his mother had no right to be so disrespectful to her. He has put all his emotional energy into becoming his wife's defender and champion. And there is nothing wrong with that.

But notice this.

One of his Inner Child's core emotional triggers has been activated – rejection. However, over the next two days, Sean does not take time to process what he is genuinely experiencing emotionally. Instead, he will continue to distract himself from feeling the pain of rejection by being angry at his mother for disrespecting his wife. So, what happens?

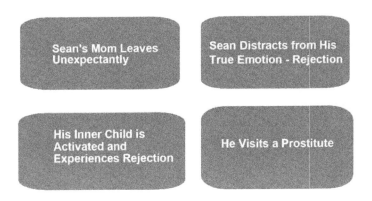

You guessed. Sean is in a hotel room two days after Christmas with a prostitute. While Sean held back and acknowledged his genuine emotions, his Inner Child had been zeroing in on them. He is sickened and sad that his mommy would turn her back on him again – and on Christmas Day! You see, Sean's Inner Child still feels invisible. And he cannot be distracted by the pain Sean's wife is feeling. He is too busy dealing with his own hurt.

When Sean's Inner Child sensed rejection, the risk barometer for acting out increased dramatically. Sean ultimately gives in to his PSBs because he does not take the time after experiencing an adverse event (mom's leaving) to slow everything down and process what has happened. And because he fails to do so, he cannot identify the emotional pain his Inner Child feels – rejection.

Over time, the hurt and pain being experienced by the Child lead Sean to fantasize and eventually succumb to his Inner Child's need for escape – visiting a prostitute. If Sean had been aware of his Child's mood and had engaged with him to process the emotional pain, the likelihood of running to a prostitute for comfort would have significantly diminished.

WHAT WENT WRONG?

During counseling, Sean received training to help ensure he reduces the risk of succumbing to his PSBs by:

- Identifying potential negative events as they occur
- Engaging his Inner Child to identify core emotional triggers that may be activated
- Sitting with and grieving the "true" emotional pain of his Inner Child
- Slowing everything down to allow cognitive thinking "wise mind" to prevail over the Child's emotionally based thinking
- Taking power away from the Child by becoming the "smart" decision-maker
- Making healthier decisions

CHRONIC LONELINESS

If no one is paying attention to you, one of the most severe consequences is loneliness. Dr. Stacey M. Solomon of the University of Virginia points out that children who endure chronic loneliness can suffer profound consequences.

"Along with increasing a child's vulnerability, chronic childhood loneliness is cause for concern; the consequences potentially have devastating long-term effects," says Dr. Solomon. "Childhood loneliness has been linked to academic failure, truancy, dropping out of school, and juvenile delinquency as well as mental health problems such as depression, suicide, hostility, alcoholism, poor self-concept, and psychosomatic illnesses."

For a child to develop strong ego strength, they must receive a positive response to a critical question — *"Do I belong."* We cannot underestimate the importance of knowing others accept, love, and support us. This comes in the form of parents and siblings who provide unconditional love and acceptance. It is found in discovering a secure place and position among peers, where you thrive, knowing you fit in and are not judged.

IF YOU ARE NOT AWARE YOUR INNER CHILD HAS BEEN ACTIVATED, HE WILL RUN THE SHOW – AND IT WILL NOT BE PRETTY

However, when these events do not occur, kids feel unwanted and undesired. Like the Bored Child, they experience a sense of loneliness and isolation, even when surrounded by people. They feel left out and question what is wrong with them that others do not express an interest or concern.

The result for some of these kids is they develop an unquenchable desire for attention that, in turn, provides self-soothing. To meet this need for attention, they may often partake in elaborate fantasies, positioning themselves as popular, successful, and the envy of others. Some exaggerate their accomplishments or engage in over-the-top bragging and storytelling to get noticed. In some cases, it is common for these disregarded children to participate in negative behaviors to get attention. As the old saying goes – *"bad attention is better than no attention."*

THE NEED GOES ON

As an adult, the need to be noticed does not fade. For example, even if this guy is engaged in a healthy relationship with a partner who showers him with attention, it may not be enough to prevent him from being captivated by the new, flirty woman in the office. While he may feel noticed by his wife, his Inner Child is fearful the attention will not last (since it never did when he was younger). Therefore, the hunt begins for the backup plan.

Sean's Inner Child is drawn to people – especially women – who notice him like a moth is drawn to a flame. Gravitating toward women who demonstrate interest has become a compulsive reaction for a man who spent too many years not being pursued by people. But it is not unusual for men like Sean to quench their thirst for attention by simultaneously becoming involved in numerous relationships. The attention they receive from multiple women provides an adrenaline rush that keeps them actively seeking more. For these men, sometimes, one is never enough.

Sean's unhealthy need for attention was fueled by the woman who should have demonstrated what real emotional bonding looked like – his mom. His unmet need for attachment to his mother has made it difficult for him to say no to any woman who expresses an interest in him.

"Although I have been with many women since getting married, I have never sought after any of them," he said. "They would make the first move, which was the most thrilling part. Knowing someone is pursuing me gets my adrenaline soaring."

The adrenaline Sean refers to is partially brought on by releasing endorphins, protein molecules that flood the brain and generate excitement and elation. Endorphins bear a likeness to morphine in that both occupy the same brain receptors. Now you understand why Sean feels like he is soaring when a woman pursues him – he is feeling no pain.

KID TALK

The Inner Child who cries out for attention needs to hear from you that he is not the problem. Use "wise mind" and rational thinking to show him many circumstances in which he felt rejection, whether it was due to the insensitivity of others or circumstances that did not permit others to spend time with him. Point out to him current relationships where individuals notice him. If he struggles to accept this, the problem may be that you are isolating too much and not seeking engagement with others because it results in too much discomfort and requires much energy.

Heap words of praise on the Child and let him know he was a good kid. Help him to feel unique, valued, and loved. Finally, assure him you can manage the situation and will be sure to protect him from unsafe people. Help him to build trust in you. In fact, you probably will be the only person he ever trusts.

Core Emotional Triggers
of the Unnoticed Inner Child

This is only a partial list, and you may identify additional triggers.
Remember, his emotions occur based on the way he perceives a
current situation. However, his perception of evens may be inccurate.

I feel rejected	I am alone
I do not belong	I am ignored
I am forgotten	I am invisible
I feel empty	I feel abandoned

What Core Emotional Triggers did you select?

TAKE A MOMENT: If you resonated with the Unnoticed Child, how do you believe it originated? Think back to Sean's childhood. Can you recall aspects of childhood that may have influenced your need for attention? Try to get in touch and talk with your Inner Child. Do not be discouraged if you are not successful immediately.

CHAPTER 6

Reason 3: The Unaffirmed Child

"Sticks and stones will break my bones, but names will never hurt me. This is a lie. What we say matters. The unkind things we communicate can spoil the best of relationships; even with the deepest of regrets...what lingers is a stain of hurt that may fade but will never truly go away."

—Jason Versey, Author

The old saying about sticks and stones is flawed and stupid. As you know, words can be as destructive or even more so than a physical attack. And while damaging words thrown in the direction of an adult can be painful, those same words hurdled at a child can cause confusion and permanent psychological harm.

A child expects unconditional love and acceptance, which starts in the arms of a nurturing mother and father. This positive affirmation, in turn, leads to the creation of strong and healthy self-esteem.

But in many cases, kids do not receive the necessary affirmation to develop healthy self-worth. And sometimes, they receive the opposite – extensive criticism – leading to troubling consequences.

Take the case of Lee, who grew up in a home with a teenage mother, a drug-addicted father, and a younger sister. As you can imagine, Lee's home life was engulfed in chaos and turmoil. His mother, practically a child herself, struggled to focus on caring for her kids. She still wanted to be a carefree young adult and often found herself bored and restless. Meanwhile, his father struggled to stay employed due to his drug addiction, which led him to be unreliable. As a result, finances were always an issue, and the family often lived on government assistance. As children, Lee and his sister faced constant verbal and physical abuse from both parents. And while physical abuse given out by his father – especially when his dad was high – was extensive – the verbal abuse Lee endured at the hands of his mother was more memorable and cutting.

"She had no filter," Lee said during one of our earlier sessions. "Whatever she was thinking came out of her mouth. She used profanity in every sentence, and the name-calling was relentless. If you didn't know my name and were around us, after a while, you would have thought it was 'stupid f---.'"

A Child Expects Unconditional Love and Acceptance, Which Starts in the Arms of a Nurturing Mother and Father

"I could sense my mom resented my sister and me at an early age," he continued. "She was too young to have children and had a hard life. I want to forgive her, but I still have nightmares of the awful words she threw at me."

Lee started viewing pornography at age 14 when he came across his father's collection and discovered it served as a pleasant escape from the anxious home environment.

"He had a pretty extensive collection, and some of it was very hardcore," Lee described. "I was incredibly careful to ensure I didn't get caught sneaking it, although that was difficult since we lived in a trailer, and he was often home. But whenever I could get my hands on some, I would go out in the woods and get lost for hours viewing the photos."

But even with pornography as an outlet to help him withdraw, Lee could not escape his mother's constant berating.

"I remember when I was 11, a friend was visiting, and my mom attempted to show me physical affection, which rarely happened,"

recalled Lee. "But thinking she was going to hit me, I jerked away. So, what did she do? She slapped me across the face and called me a piece of s... She continued to scream at me and told my friend to get the f*** out of her house. I was mortified. I remember spending the night in the woods repeatedly masturbating to get the scene out of my head.

"Although I worked hard to stay out of trouble, I was never good enough for either of them," he said with his eyes focused on the floor. "And although I hated the criticism, it didn't bother me as much as the lack of praise. I tried and tried to please them with my actions, but I never received a positive word of affirmation. I would bring home a good report card or win an award at school, and no one cared. I was not important. What was important to my mom was non-stop entertainment television and my dad getting his next drug hit. Other than that, nothing else mattered, especially my sister or me."

WHAT GOES WRONG

Although most scenarios are not as extreme as the one Lee endured, men who abuse sex to feel affirmed grow up receiving little in the way of praise and perhaps a great deal of criticism. But the result is the same – low self-worth.

Affirmation is necessary for individuals to believe they are unconditionally loved and accepted by others. Without experiencing these essential emotional bonds, individuals are destined to struggle in relationships because of their poor self-image.

A child who receives little in the way of affirmation will believe nothing he does is good enough. He will always feel he falls short in his efforts to please others and does not get the opportunity to learn how to feel proud of his achievements.

Later, as an adult, even if he has achieved enormous success in the academic or professional world, his Inner Child will believe his accomplishments are tainted. He may feel like a fraud.

In receiving little praise and accolades, this individual lacks confidence; therefore, he may be unwilling to take risks. His Inner Child will push him to hide in the back of the room and become just another face in the crowd. That is a safe place. It is safe because no one can discover he does not measure up.

"I'm always fearful my co-workers are going to think I am incompetent, and I will get fired," said Randolph, who recently was named employee of the month at the medical device firm where he is employed. "My anxiety becomes extremely high when someone approaches me with a question. I freeze up in fear I will give them the wrong answer.

WITHOUT EXPERIENCING AFFIRMATION AS A CHILD, AN INDIVIDUAL IS DESTINED TO STRUGGLE IN RELATIONSHIPS DUE TO HIS POOR SELF-IMAGE

"Then they will see me for who I am, a fraud," he continued. Randolph graduated from one of the country's leading technical universities and has never been fired during his 14-year career. In fact, it has been just the opposite. He is continuously being recognized with promotions and bonuses.

His lack of confidence comes from a father who consistently delivered the message, *"You don't know what you're doing."* Randolph has carried that message with him into his adult world, and despite this occupational success, he believes he is not worthy of recognition. How does an intelligent and analytical individual like Randolph buy into the irrational belief that he is flawed? You guessed it — his Inner Child.

You see, "Little R" still hears daddy's critical voice pointing out negative after negative about his son's ability to succeed. So, even when Randolph receives accolades for a job well done, Little R is saying, *"Who are you kidding? We just got lucky again."*

Starting at an early age, this individual reeks of shame and believes he does not meet expectations. His shame will have devastating consequences as he becomes a teenager and adult, leading him to take several paths to escape the negative emotions that lurk beneath the surface.

- First, there is the child who becomes an angry, resentful, and defiant adult and finds it difficult to experience joy and pleasure in anything or anyone. His shame leaks out in anger, thus allowing this man to hand out criticism. "Nothing can make my husband happy," said Camilla, speaking of Lawrence, who has struggled with PSBs for nearly 25 years. "He is critical of everyone and everything. He is just like his father. And I have come to hate him." Although these men feel weak and lack confidence, their Inner Child has them hiding behind the façade of a bully. The Child is on the offensive, and his goal is to hurt others before being hurt. In this scenario, the destructive cycle experienced as a child continues.

- This adult feels weak and lacks confidence, but instead of hiding behind a façade, his Inner Child simply allows him to fade into the background. His shame leads to withdrawing and not taking risks. He will struggle to identify and express his emotions. In fact, children of overly critical parents show fewer emotional facial expressions, according to a 2018 research study conducted at Binghamton University, State University in New York. *"We know from previous research that people tend to avoid things that make them uncomfortable, anxious, or sad because such feelings are aversive. We also know that children with a critical parent are more likely to use avoidant coping strategies when they are in distress than children without a critical parent,"* said Kiera James, a graduate student of psychology at Binghamton University and lead author of the paper.

- Some children who deal with chronic criticism become adults who fulfill the negative prophecy drilled into their heads at an early age. Their shame is on display as they give in to the belief they are worthless. These adults who endured ruthless criticism as children struggle in many aspects of life, including career and relationships, because their Inner Child continues to believe they are undeserving of happiness or success. This guy also could be labeled as over-sensitive by others.

"Brandon is one the neediest men I have ever met, and it drives me crazy," said Nicole, whose husband's pornography viewing shifted to chat room sexting in the past year. "I have to watch everything I say and how I say it to ensure he doesn't feel criticized. Because if he does, he will start pouting."

These once verbally beaten down men demonstrate their hidden shame of feeling unloved by engaging in an unending quest to find love and acceptance. However, their approach to this chase is made in destructive ways. Some turn to sex as an outlet to find affirmation, while others use control to ensure those who love them do not abandon or criticize them. As in the other scenarios, the Inner Child is desperate for unconditional love and acceptance.

LEE'S INNER CHILD

Life for Lee has not been pleasant. He has been divorced three times and is currently single, and his PSBs are still in full swing. Today, at 56, Lee frequents strip clubs and solicits prostitutes three times a week.

"I'm a loser and always have been," he said during one of our sessions. "My mom was right when she said I would never amount to anything. That is why I haven't gotten married again. I know I would mess up the next one, too."

Lee's Inner Child is full of self-loathing. The constant beratement suffered as a child, and the lack of affirming words have left him depressed and defeated. His Inner Child serves as a continuous recording that plays in the back of

Lee's mind, filling his head with various negative narratives echoed by his mother decades earlier.

Lee's Inner Child is triggered by events that make him feel inadequate or worthless, to name a few. Therefore, the Child has no hope and seeks temporary relief from the emotional pain by engaging in highly stimulating and risky sexual activities. He does not care if he ends up with a sexually transmitted disease or is robbed during a session with a hooker. In Lee's mind, he would deserve it. So, what if he blows his entire paycheck on strippers and continues to make his dire financial situation bleaker? The Child does not care about anything but comfort and does that by escaping from his emotional pain by abusing sex.

As you can see, Lee's Inner Child is scared and seeking safety at any cost. Please note not all men who select the Unaffirmed Child have an Inner Child like Lee. As I pointed out earlier in this chapter, the development of the Inner Child can take many different paths depending on the environment he was raised in and the intensity of the trauma and/or neglect.

It is essential to understand whether these men act out through sexting, affairs, massage parlors, or pornography; they are engaged in a fantasy in which they believe they are desired. However, this is a false sense of emotional intimacy.

These men desire real intimacy, but to make that commitment is frightening. Their Inner Child recalls being rejected and fears reliving the painful experiences again. Therefore, reaching out to create authentic relationships — even with their spouse — is scary because they may not respond positively to their invitation. It is easier to remain present than to engage.

When you fear rejection, one of the easiest ways to find companionship is through online connections in chat rooms, social media, or virtual apps. The ability to hide behind an anonymous facade empowers those who feel insecure about being accepted by others. If you are rejected by one, you move on to another until someone says, *"Yes, I want to spend time with you."*

Another activity these individuals may engage in is called "trolling." They will search social media outlets such as Facebook and LinkedIn to view profiles of people they find attractive. They rarely contact individuals but instead experience fantasies regarding the positive impact those people could have on their lives.

GOD'S GIFT TO WOMEN

Some men become very observant of the women around them, always looking for subtle clues to determine if a woman is interested. Other men "groom" potential sex partners by offering to serve as a mentor or lend a sympathetic ear.

They also discover being a good sex partner can lead to endless praise and affirmation. This will lead them to seek recognition from others based on their ability to provide sexual satisfaction and pleasure to their partners. They will focus more on pleasuring their partner than their fulfillment to receive recognition.

These men often invest time and energy learning various sexual techniques to enhance their love-making skills. While their goal may seem to provide sexual satisfaction and pleasure to their partners, the aim is to obtain affirmation and praise.

In extreme cases, these men believe they are God's gift to women and cheat women if they do not allow them to experience the physical pleasure they can deliver.

"When I had sex, my attention was 100% on determining if the woman I was with was feeling sexually satisfied," said Ezra, a womanizer who estimates he had sex with more than 500 women. "It was all about how many orgasms I could give a woman. It was like I was in a contest with myself. I knew if I rocked their world, they would be singing my praises, and that's what I wanted more than anything."

TOO MUCH AFFIRMATION?

Another scenario that can lead to the development of the Unaffirmed Child is when a young boy receives an overabundance of affirmation as a child and teenager. This praise could be related to performance efforts such as academics or athletics. The affirmation is sometimes given because of the child's attractive appearance.

Despite the rationale, these individuals become accustomed to being in the limelight and having people deliver vast volumes of accolades. However, as some children age, peers catch up academically and athletically — sometimes surpassing them. For children praised for their appearance, sometimes getting older brings about facial changes that are not complimentary.

With these changes, the limelight fades, and the laurels become sparse, if not at all. This leaves these children hungry to return to times when they were set apart and honored for their achievements. But the spotlight no longer shines on them. Their Unaffirmed Child has been created.

KID TALK

The Inner Child who struggles to feel affirmed needs to process painful moments. The key is to listen and understand the depth of the pain and the negative narratives he believes. This Child will struggle to believe what you are telling him because he has dwelled on a list of negative beliefs that will be challenging to overcome.

You need patience with this Child. You need to identify past pain points and learn to sit with them before shifting to using your "wise mind" and rational thinking to deal with the child's hurt in a productive manner.

You will need to offer praise and encouragement. Point out victories achieved during recovery and credit the Child for working with you. Think of yourselves as teammates.

Helping the Inner Child who struggles with a lack of affirmation is not a short-term process — in fact, overcoming any of these reasons why takes dedication, commitment, and time. But a child who receives little positive affirmation and much criticism has been set up for failure as an adult. A healthy adult is groomed as a child to believe he is special and has value. When he instead receives the opposite, his self-worth takes an enormous hit, and the process of rebuilding his confidence can be challenging. Not impossible. Challenging.

Core Emotional Triggers of the Unaffirmed Inner Child

This is only a partial list, and you may identify additional triggers. Remember, his emotions occur based on the way he perceives a current situation. However, his perception of evens may be inccurate.

I am a dissapointment

I am a failure

I feel incompentent

I am stupid

I feel Insulted

I am unheard

I feel small

I am not lovable

I feel inferior

I am a mistake

What Core Emotional Triggers did you select?

TAKE A MOMENT: What led to your need for constant affirmation if you resonated with the Unaffirmed Child? Was it based on a lack of praise, constant criticism, or praise that faded? Where did it originate? Take time to write out your thoughts.

CHAPTER 7

Reason 4: The Emotionally Voided Child

"He thought about all the holes in him, the blank places, the voids where others felt things. When it came down to it, he was just a screen, more empty than solid, his emotions blowing through him, only angry catching and holding."

— J.R. Ward, Author

"He doesn't talk."

It is a comment I often hear from women who have lived with men struggling with PSBs. Take Maria, for example. *"It's so frustrating to live with someone who can't carry on a simple conversation,"* she said, looking in the direction of Jack, her husband of 14 years. *"It's a chore to get him to socialize, and*

when we do, he barely interacts with other people. He may latch onto one person the entire night. And when he's at home, he is here but doesn't interact with the kids or me.

"And while all of this is annoying, to discover he is a full-blown porn addict just adds to the hurt," she continued shaking her head in disgust and bewilderment. "He can watch that filth but can't connect with his family. I don't know what to do with all of this. I feel lost."

Unfortunately, Maria's experience with Jack often happens with those who struggle with PSBs. I estimate nine of 10 men who come into my office for help are also emotionally undeveloped and deal with a low emotional IQ. So, what does a low emotional IQ look like? Let us explore this personality trait that gets many men in marital trouble.

A man possessing a low emotional IQ will find it difficult to process and express his own emotions while also struggling to recognize and adequately manage the feelings of others. They become exasperated and anxious when put in environments that require them to give or accept an emotional connection. Therefore, they have learned how to avoid engaging in emotional intimacy.

WHEN WE CUT OFF EMOTIONS, WE KILL A PART OF OURSELVES

In fact, many would not recognize emotional intimacy if it ran them over. Here are some behaviors you can expect from an individual with a low emotional IQ.

1. They cannot identify what they are "truly" feeling. Sure, these individuals can tell you when they are angry, sad, afraid, lonely, or happy. But everyone can experience those emotions, and they are utilized to protect us from dealing with deeper and more vulnerable emotions. Individuals with a strong emotional IQ can drill down from the initial emotions and identify their deeper feelings. However, those with a low emotional IQ cannot process and describe their more robust feelings. For example, an angry person may actually be feeling dismissed or cheated. But instead of recognizing their genuine emotion and expressing the hurt associated with it, they react in anger.

2. Even if this individual can determine his real emotions, he will struggle to express them. Men with low emotional IQs were never taught how to process and communicate feelings appropriately. Therefore, they prefer to keep their emotions to themselves. Somewhere along the line, they receive the message sharing your feelings results in trouble.

3. What is most annoying for partners of guys with a low emotional IQ is their inability to recognize and effectively deal with the emotions of others. These men cannot read people's emotional signs, especially non-verbal cues. They also lack the ability to be empathic listeners; instead, they try to fix, minimize, or ignore the problem.

4. These men tend to shift emotional conversations toward themselves. For example, if his wife says, "It

was a crazy day, and my head is spinning," instead of asking her what left her mentally exhausted, he will say something like, "I know what you're feeling. I also had an insane day." He does not pick up the fact she is trying to be vulnerable and looking to engage in conversation to get a sympathetic ear. His inability to do this will send her the indirect message, "I don't care about your day," which is not what he meant to do.

5. A man with a low emotional IQ may find making and maintaining friendships difficult. Part of the reason for this is his constant desire for solitude. A man who must engage with people throughout the workday will become very drained and have little energy for his family, never mind friends. He will give the impression of being aloof, although that is not his intent. However, he may have friends in some cases, but these relationships are kept on a 10,000-foot level and rarely, if ever, result in emotionally meaningful conversations.

"He is so dry when it comes to sharing anything that remotely reassembles a feeling," said Brittany. "I have never met a man who can be so out-of-touch with how he feels. It's frustrating not knowing what is going on in his head. And I always expect the worst when left in the dark."

Brittany's comments about her husband, Tommy, highlight a key aspect of men who abuse sex. With the avalanche of sexual thoughts spinning through their minds throughout the day, they spend an incredible amount of time in their heads. Therefore, women feel lonely and isolated, even when their men spend time with them.

These men have their heads buried so deep in the sand that it is not unusual for them to troll or contact other women on their tablets or smartphones when the wife is in the same room. Doesn't that sound like insanity? It is for individuals who are thinking rationally about the circumstances. But not so for the man with PSBs. He is so wrapped up in the excitement of the hunt that he is oblivious that he is in danger of getting caught. Not to mention, he is engaging in practices causing tremendous emotional harm to the woman he says he loves.

A Man's Inability to Experience and Process Emotional Pain Can Result in Him Using Sex As An Escape

Having been a guy with a low emotional IQ, I know firsthand these men have no idea what it means to be emotionally connected with another individual. We think we do. But sexual and non-sexual touch is our number one way to demonstrate emotional intimacy. Our erroneous belief is, *"You show a woman you love her by how you make her feel physically."* It is another significant complaint spouses often discuss.

"The only time he touches or acknowledges me is when he wants to have sex," said Barbara, whose husband viewed pornography and visited strip clubs regularly. "I start to cringe whenever he comes near me because I know what he wants. It leaves me feeling used, and he doesn't understand that."

But if you talk with her husband, Mario, you will get a different perspective. "Yes, I approach her physically, but that is how I know to please her," he countered. "I enjoy the sex but get more satisfaction knowing I please her. It's the way I show I care and love her, but she doesn't understand me."

And there is a good reason she does not understand. Because God did not intend for intimate relationships to be based primarily on physical intimacy. The foundation of a relationship should be built on emotional intimacy, which includes trust. We then take physical intimacy and sprinkle it in to strengthen the emotional component.

A couple who does not cultivate emotional intimacy increases the risk of infidelity seeping its way into the relationship. And their outlook for a rewarding partnership becomes shaky.

THE EMOTIONALLY VOIDED CHILD

This Inner Child HATES feeling any emotions except those that are pleasurable. Remember, his goal is always to seek comfort. The Inner Child of a man with a low emotional IQ is hypervigilant and on the alert for troubling emotions experienced internally and those expressed by others. He is on guard to sound the alarm that danger is lurking — *"Emotions are in the house, and it is time to jump ship!"*

To the Inner Child, emotions are destructive and something you should avoid at all costs. These kids were raised in homes where they saw little emotional intimacy being expressed. There was moderate or no physical touch displayed between parents or siblings. A hug or kiss was rare to find. And if it did come, it was usually quick or half-hearted. The child raised in this environment does not have the model needed to be emotionally engaging. Therefore, this Inner Child will be severely disadvantaged when dealing with emotions and learning to connect intimately with others.

In her book *Running on Empty: Overcome Your Childhood Emotional Neglect*, Dr. Jonice Webb provides several explanations for developing a low emotional IQ.

- This is the child whose parents did not teach emotional processing skills because they struggled to identify their own emotions. Feelings were never discussed in this home; if any were presented, they were quickly shut down or dismissed. "When your prom date stands you up, your family shows their support by making an effort never to speak of it," says Dr. Webb in providing an example of what this child went through at home. "Or they tease you about it relentlessly, never seeming to notice or care how very mortified you are. The result is that these individuals don't learn to be self-aware," she continues. "They don't learn that their feelings are real or important. And they are not taught how to feel, sit with, talk about, or express emotions."

- Other kids struggle with their emotional IQ because their parents were not good at managing and controlling their own emotions; therefore, they were unable to teach children how to manage and control their own. "When you get in trouble at school for calling your teacher 'a jerk,' your parents do not ask you what was going on or why you lost your temper that way," Dr. Webb explains. "They don't teach you how you could have handled that situation differently. Instead, they ground you, or they yell at you, or they blame it on your teacher, letting you off the hook. The result is these kids don't learn how to control or manage their feelings or how to manage difficult situations."

- For these children, it is about receiving the wrong message about themselves and the world due to insensitive behavior from parents and family members who simply are emotionally clueless. "Take, for example, that your parents act as if you're lazy because they haven't noticed that it's your anxiety that holds you back from doing things," says Dr. Webb. "The result is these individuals go into adulthood with the wrong voices in their heads. 'You're lazy,' 'You're weak,' say the Voices of Low Emotional Intelligence at every opportunity."

The Inner Child with low emotional intelligence lacks awareness of his surroundings and people. They have spent life running with their heads down, oblivious to the rest of the world, while stuck in their thoughts. To become emotionally intimate, they will need to learn how to keep their heads upright to be aware of the needs and desires of those around them and recognize opportunities to engage in genuine community.

FEAR OF REJECTION

Men who grow up not learning to engage in a healthy way emotionally with others will often become anxious when placed in social environments. They lack the confidence to be able to carry on conversations. More importantly, they subconsciously worry about rejection if they allow people to get too emotionally close. So, what is the Inner Child's solution? The following:

- Keep people at a distance
- Learn to be present but not to engage
- Maintain a low profile and stay out of sight
- Do not share thoughts and opinions unless asked
- Always keep your answers short and to the point
- Too many spoken words can get you in trouble

When I talk to men about emotional intimacy, most give a facial expression like a deer caught in headlights. They have no idea what is about to hit them. They only know it sounds dangerous. They would not know emotional intimacy if it hit them in the head. What is ironic is men crave emotional intimacy and connection – they do not realize it. Read what author Eric Armstrong says about this in his blog *Tree Light*.

"A porn/sex addiction is a practice that produces intense pleasure but impedes the ability to create and maintain a healthy sex life. Like heroin, it gets into your system, stimulating the pleasure pathways that are part of your biology, but without satiating the real need that lies deep within all of us for the comfort and security of love, of family."

Todd is an excellent example of a man who struggles to achieve an emotional connection.

"I have no idea what to do when my wife comes to me seeking support because she is struggling to deal with her mother and sister," said Todd, who struggles with PSBs and has been married for five years. "And if she starts to cry, I freeze up and want to run out of the room. I know I'm going to say the wrong thing. It's so overwhelming for me; my mind goes blank. Then she gets angry with me for not saying anything or attempting to comfort her. I want to, but I don't have a clue how to do it."

Like many men who struggle with PSBs, Todd is extremely limited in what he can give and receive through emotional intimacy. This can be extremely frustrating to a spouse or children looking for connection and engagement.

If you are not taught how to engage with others in a healthy manner, you will most likely feel uncomfortable and awkward when placed in circumstances that require you to interact.

In their best-selling book *How We Love*, Milan and Kay Yerkovich point out we do not learn to love when we start dating or get married. We learn to love in our family of origin.

"What bothers you most about your spouse is undoubtedly related to painful experiences from childhood and lack of training in addressing the true challenges of marriage. Your marriage problems did not begin in your marriage! You and your spouse are doing the dance steps you learned in childhood. For each of you, a pattern of relating was set in motion long before you met."

So, what happens to a boy who does not witness healthy love growing up because his parents are too distracted or negligent in engaging with him? He most likely shuts off his emotional pipeline and fails to develop the social skills needed to be an affectionate and attentive partner. And he will be quick to withdraw when emotions emerge during conversations. A big complaint I hear from the wives of men who struggle with PSBs is they are too quick to withdraw from the family.

WE DO NOT LEARN TO LOVE WHEN WE START DATING OR GET MARRIED; WE LEARN TO LOVE IN OUR FAMILY OF ORIGIN

"It's like clockwork," says Mara, whose husband Chuck has utilized online pornography since its inception in the mid-90s. "One minute he's with us, and the next minute he's burying himself in his phone or other electronics. It's frustrating because it communicates to the kids and me that we are not important or annoying. It's like something clicks in his brain, and he runs away from us."

A vital component of a man's sexual recovery is to learn techniques to reduce the anxiety he experiences when emotions arise so he can remain engaged instead of simply

154

being present. Unbelievably, this is sometimes more difficult for a man to accomplish than managing their PSBs.

"I just don't know what to say," said Andy, a 40-year-old who has dealt with sexual integrity issues since high school. "When my wife mentions emotional topics, I just freeze. Then, I ended up trying to fix the situation. But that just makes her angry. I feel like I cannot win. I hate dealing with emotions."

Managing the Inner Child's fear of emotions is critical for your recovery and establishing healthy, long-lasting relationships. Fear is what got you in this mess, to begin with — you are not in touch with your emotions, especially those that are painful and uncomfortable. This fear can be managed, but the first step is recognizing it exists. Then, you can take steps to address it by committing to be vulnerable and share with someone safe.

You must take a risk.

Let us be honest; it is not like you are unfamiliar with risk-taking. You probably took many risks when it involved your PSBs. Those were risks that did or could have cost you dearly. The danger we are discussing is extremely different and can result in tremendous positive dividends. You may finally understand what it is like to be alive. What does that sound like?

KID TALK

So, what does your Emotionally Voided Child need to hear from you? Here are some practical tools to teach and comfort this Child. This Child does not believe emotions are safe, so you must provide him with insights about the benefits of emotions. Let him know that sharing feelings can ease burdens and decrease the chances of experiencing stress-related problems like muscle aches and tension headaches. Remember, his goal is comfort, so let him know what well-being can be found in sharing emotions.

He does not believe people are safe. The Kid is frightened that sharing emotions will result in rejection. This comes back to the concept of taking risks. Let him know you will "go slow" when it comes to sharing emotions to see how individuals react. Over time, you will expand sharing with those who prove trustworthy. Discuss how being emotionally vulnerable can help strengthen relationships and allow you to experience more love and life.

Your Inner Child may have received the message that being emotional is a sign of weakness, and feelings should never be expressed. His worldview is emotions can do nothing but get you in trouble.

Now, while you cannot guarantee your emotions will always be validated whenever you express them, your emphasis must focus on the importance of empowerment despite the potential negative outcome. Sharing means we have taken control. Your Inner Child will like that message.

If you want more information regarding how men can be emotionally undeveloped and possess a low emotional IQ, check out my book, Why Men Struggle to Love: Overcoming Relational Blind Spots. There, you will discover the 14 Blind Spots that keep men from forming healthy and intimate relationships and why being sober is not enough.

Core Emotional Triggers
of the Emotionally Voided Inner Child

This is only a partial list, and you may identify additional triggers.
Remember, his emotions occur based on the way he perceives a
current situation. However, his perception of evens may be incurate.

I am a dissapointment	I am always wrong
I am scared	I am not important
I feel overwhelmed	I do not know what to feel
I am confused	I am inadequate
I feel lost	I feel nothing

What Core Emotional Triggers did you select?

TAKE A MOMENT: What messages did you receive directly and indirectly from your parents, siblings, peers, and others about handling emotions? Was anyone available to help you sort through your feelings and guide you on what they represented? If not, how do you believe this negatively impacts you today?

CHAPTER 8
Reason 5: The Need for Control Child

"Fear is a response to actual danger that is right here, right now, while anxiety is a concern for events that only might happen — events that may be unpredictable and that you may lack control over."

—Alex Korb, Author

Harry was dealt a bad hand. To say his childhood was chaotic would be an understatement. He was the first of four children, and among his siblings was a brother with autism. His father suffered from chronic depression that prevented him from being steadily employed. Instead, if you needed to find Harry's dad, you had to look no further than the bedroom, where he spent endless hours watching television.

Meanwhile, his mother was forced to work two jobs to support the family. And when she was not working, you could typically find her sitting at a barstool at the tavern across the street from their apartment. A Hallmark family, it was not.

As the oldest child, it naturally fell upon Harry to become his siblings' caregiver at the expense of his childhood. Due to home life demands, Harry had to forgo youthful activities most kids enjoy. He traded in friends and school experiences for the role of a surrogate parent. Harry would miss out on being a child and teenager. He suffered a lost childhood.

"I was an adult way before my time," he said with a muffled voice and a terrible sense of sadness. "But there was no one there to care for the others. Dad was always locked in his bedroom, and Mom was never home. No one ever told me I had to care for my siblings; I just took it upon myself. However, I knew If I didn't step up, we probably would have been sent to foster care, and I couldn't allow that to happen.

"But in reality, I was dying every day," he continued as he slowly monitored his words. "I am not sure how I got schoolwork done with everything else I needed to do. But I did. Looking back, it seems impossible for a kid to raise three other kids. But that was my life. There was nothing else."

Handling the responsibilities of an adult while trying to be a productive student caused Harry chronic anxiety, a condition he still deals with today. Facing an environment that would be challenging for two parents was overwhelming for the young boy, who often felt over his head trying to manage a household, schoolwork, and child-rearing responsibilities.

YOU LOSE CONTROL WHEN YOU GIVE UP YOUR POWER

"I was always worried I would mess up and something would happen to one of my brothers or my sister," he recalled. "Especially Arthur, who had autism. He was a handful, and I had no idea how to handle him or what was wrong with him. I didn't know what autism was. It was scary.

"I felt as though I was constantly living in a state of fear," he continued. "Whether I would pass my classes or ensure everyone was fed. There was ALWAYS something that needed to be done and ALWAYS something that I worried I wasn't doing. I have been on anti-anxiety meds most of my adult life."

SEEKING ESCAPES

The chaos in the noisy, unorganized, and cluttered apartment often left Harry feeling he failed in his self-appointed responsibilities. Harry thought he was disappointing his mother, father, siblings, and himself. It was a tremendous emotional burden placed on a young boy's shoulders, who often thought about running away to escape his feelings of failure. You may equate a chaotic environment with an abusive environment, but that is not always the case. Yes, abusive environments are chaotic, but not all chaotic environments are abusive. Instead, they are viewed as neglectful.

Harry eventually found two escapes from the emotional pandemonium that swirled through his head and the endless responsibilities that faced him – control and pornography. He learned that to manage the hellish environment, control was essential. Out of self-preservation, Harry became a drill sergeant. He established a rigid and uncompromising climate in the home and among his siblings to create stability. Each was given tasks that needed to be completed daily, and there was no room for non-compliance.

MEN WILL USE CONTROL TO SEEK SANCTUARY FROM THE CHRONIC EMOTIONAL DISTRESS THEY FACE

"I was at a loss because no one was showing me how to raise kids," Harry said as he leaned back on the couch, seeming exhausted just talking about the situation. "I had to get them to listen to me, especially Arthur, so I decided to become a hard-head with all of them. I was determined not to fail."

With his new approach to running the home, Harry addressed non-compliance with rules and punishment, including physical attacks. Soon, his younger siblings understood a new sheriff was in town. They soon discovered doing chores was a better option than beatings. And while Harry hated who he was becoming, he saw no other solution.

Harry ran a tight ship at home as he entered his teen years, but it came at a high cost. His brothers and sister feared and hated him. He had no social life, and his grades at school were suffering. While he could institute structure at home that created some sense of control, Harry's anxiety was still running amok. Enter escape number two.

At age 13, Harry came across some of his father's pornographic magazines. The images he saw were incredibly stimulating for a child whose mind focused mainly on dealing with the next crisis. He soon discovered pornography served as a tremendous distraction to the frenzy he was surrounded by at home.

"It sounds crazy, but pornography was like a light in all of the darkness," he explained. "It was one of the few times I could recall life was pleasurable. Looking back, I know it was wrong, but I needed it back then. It kept me sane."

Harry soon discovered he could control his anxiety by taking breaks to view pornography and masturbate. The invigoration of pornography kept at bay distressful and uneasy feelings and thoughts that continuously plagued Harry. It became a source of relief for a young boy put in circumstances he should never have faced. His parents' failure to carry out their responsibilities led him to addictive behaviors that would later cause severe issues in his romantic relationships.

Men like Harry use sexual activity to maintain stability and provide a feeling of security. They use control to remain safe. Safe from what you may ask? Good question. They seek sanctuary from chronic emotional distress they experience in the form of anxiety or depression. In most cases, these individuals have no clue regarding the true nature of their emotional turmoil.

UNREALIZED STRESS

Listen to Harry today as an adult; he will tell you his anxiety is more a sense of restlessness. That is why he continually stays busy running from one activity to the next. But he has no idea from what he is running. Two core emotional triggers his Inner Child seeks to escape are *"I'm a disappointment"* and *"I don't measure up."* But again, Harry is unaware of these emotional triggers that activate his Inner Child. Instead, he thinks his hectic schedule is nothing more than an attempt to keep his life organized and controlled. However, his life is anything but harmonious.

After high school, Harry left home and found a low-level construction job. His strong work ethic helped him succeed in the workplace, and he later started his own business. His need for control led to financial success, which was good.

But his personal life has been anything but prosperous. Harry has been divorced twice and is working hard to keep together a third marriage hanging on by a string. Why has he experienced so much destruction in his relationship world? Because he still struggles with PSBs and has betrayed every woman he has ever dated or married.

Harry acts out regularly with sexual activities ranging from high-class escorts to sexual encounters in sleazy adult bookstores. If he is not focused on his business, Harry seeks sex to drown the faint, chaotic background noise (that he cannot hear) forever playing in his head that he is not good enough and failure is right around the corner.

"I have always wondered why I cheat," he said as he started to tear up. "I assumed it was a character flaw. I never knew until we started therapy that I was using sex to keep my insecurity of failing buried. I wish I had known all this earlier. It would have saved me and others a lot of grief."

HARRY'S INNER CHILD

How is this for irony? A man who is fixated on control is uncontrollable when dealing with sex.

As I have been pointing out, the rationale behind this craziness is he does not understand the true nature of his anxiousness. At his core, Harry's Inner Child is fearful and overwhelmed. He worries chaos will develop at any moment, and life will spin out of control. The Child fears failure and, therefore, directs Harry to take charge of all situations and, if necessary, use unhealthy sexual activities to distract from potential negative feelings.

For these men, there are two reasons why their Inner Child may be activated when experiencing circumstances that leave them feeling somewhat powerless. We have already reviewed one in our case study regarding Harry. His Inner Child uses control as a protective device to generate feelings that life is orderly and prevents bad things from happening. He uses sex to achieve a sense of control when faced with circumstances he cannot control.

When engaging in sexual activities, he is not thinking about anything that may seem overwhelming, therefore, Harry believes he controls all his circumstances. As we discussed with previous Inner Children, this mindset is false. He has not changed his circumstances by engaging in unwanted sexual behaviors. Instead, he has increased the likelihood of generating more trouble for himself and others. And he is certainly creating more anxiety in his life.

THE VOICELESS CHILD

Another rationale for the development of the Need for Control Child is to avoid the painful emotion of feeling micromanaged. Some kids grow up in homes governed by rules, rules, and more rules. A rigid environment can feel like a vise tightening around your throat, leaving you gasping for air. You have no say in your life and are given a limited or no voice. Life is not your own — instead, it is managed by others.

"I grew up with a military dad, and we moved a lot," said Terrell, who struggles with pornography, which escalated to video chatting until his wife walked in on him one night. "My sister and I were raised as mindless soldiers. Our opinions never mattered. The house directive was 'always obey,' which is still the case whenever I visit my parents.

"Meals lacked flavor because Dad likes bland food," he continued. "That is okay, but we all had to eat what he ate. He determined what clothes we wore, what television programs we could watch, what time we got up in the morning and went to bed. We were not allowed to voice our opinions or desires. And you don't even try to fight it because you know it's a battle you will lose."

Two Core Emotional Triggers For This Inner Child Are "I'm a Disappointment" and "I Don't Measure Up"

Terrell would retreat to his room whenever he was home, engaging in fantasy to escape the harsh environment. What started as dreams of being a superhero or achieving athletic success turned to lust after being exposed to pornography by a neighborhood friend. Fantasy gave Terrell the only form of control he could have in that stifling home. And that is still the case today.

"What I have come to learn as an adult is when I feel dismissed or sense my opinion doesn't matter, my Inner Child leads me to escape into sexual fantasy," he said, reviewing notes he had taken during counseling sessions. "I take control of the situation by generating a feeling I can do anything without being told no. I experience a powerful sense of defiance. And frankly, I liked that."

Children like Terrell are not allowed to make decisions or share their opinions. Instead, they meet the needs and wants of others to conform to the family system. While parents believe their intentions are to provide healthy guidelines required for their sons to develop into productive individuals, they are instead creating men filled with anxiety, resentment, and anger.

Growing up in a hectic or stifling environment, these men seek to control some aspect of their surroundings. Why? As the past demonstrated, they suffer the consequences when there is no control. Therefore, they believe they are preventing troubling things from occurring in their lives by taking control. In their minds, control equates with tranquility and security.

Author Andrew Bauman discusses this concept in his popular book, *The Psychology of Porn,* pointing out how the table turns when these men become adults. *"We sexualize our wounds in a desperate attempt to heal our unaddressed pain. Porn can help for a fleeting time and temporarily meet many of the core needs (love, touch, emotional attunement, pleasure, and delight) we may not have received as a child,"* writes Bauman. *"For example, if your parents were emotionally distant, you probably longed for intimate connection. Though you were powerless to control what you received or did not receive from your parents as a child, as an adult, you choose to have power and control over this deep, unmet longing for intimacy by using pornography to attempt to tend to that core wound."*

For this Inner Child, control is the glue that holds everything in place and prevents chaos. Control provides the Child with a sense of peace. All the Inner Children will do anything to obtain this peace, including pointing the adults toward bad decision-making. The Child does this because he understands sex serves as a marvelous distraction to the anxiousness occurring in the adult world. Basically, the Inner Child uses sex to obtain a false sense of security.

Why is Pseudo-Control Important?

We do not need to be in control to have comfort, which is the primary objective of our Inner Child. He recalls trying to survive in an abusive, chaotic, stoic, or rigid atmosphere experienced at home or elsewhere, such as school or in the neighborhood. And when similar circumstances arise today, he refuses to allow us to sit with those painful emotions. In his limited, emotionally focused world, maintaining control is the answer to creating stability.

"If we're in charge, bad things can't happen to us" is his worldview.

Due to our lack of awareness, we yield to our Inner Child's worldview, and the result is escaping via sex to avoid facing troubling emotions. Again, he is running the show. And we are not better because of it.

YOU ARE NOT VIEWING YOUR EMOTIONS AND THOUGHTS THROUGH THE LENS OF TRUTH WHEN YOU GIVE IN TO YOUR INNER CHILD

When you allow your Inner Child to lead, you are not viewing your emotions and thoughts through the lens of truth. Instead, you elect to listen to the distorted views of a hurt child who will seek comfort at any cost. You are listening and following an adolescent voice when you need to hear and follow a voice of wisdom.

Remember, the Inner Child does not trust people – often, the available adults were untrusting. He is somewhat paranoid and on alert for those who will try to hurt him or cannot assist him when he is suffering. To prevent that from happening, the Child, who equates control with security, will ultimately make incorrect assumptions. But then again, he does not know better – he is just a kid.

Best-selling author John Bradshaw, who wrote one of the premier books about the Inner Child, *Homecoming: Reclaiming and Healing Your Inner Child,* noted the confused mind of our young companion.

"A person who never learned to trust confuses intensity with intimacy, obsession with care, and control with security," says Bradshaw in his definition of the Inner Child.

When our Inner Child feels the comfortable state of harmony is being disrupted (via core emotional triggers), he seeks to protect himself. If we allow the Child to go unchecked, he will lead us to make emotionally charged decisions. When the Inner Child determines the action an adult should take to reduce anxiety, you can bet it will most likely lead to destructive consequences.

The first step in recovery is realizing you are not in control. The dopamine addiction has disempowered you. The key is to face our past pain and develop the coping skills required to soothe your Inner Child and empower yourself. But by doing this, we will reduce our dependency on dopamine to produce unneeded adrenaline rushes. It is time for you to start running the show.

Kid Talk

Here are some practical tools to teach and comfort the Inner Child who lacks control. Remember, we are trying to soothe and not criticize or belittle him. You want to determine your Inner Child's negative narratives. If you recall, negative narratives are the lies our Inner Child believes about us. You start by dialoguing with the Child to uncover the negative narratives he believes.

Once you have determined them, ponder how they may have developed. Where did he first hear those narratives? Who or what was responsible for their development? Once you have that vital information, you can start placing each negative narrative in front of the mirror of truth, which is asking yourself, *"Although I feel this way, what is reality?"* and *"Is this an accurate description of myself?"* If you answer yes, back up your belief with facts. If you still believe the negative narrative, turn to someone you can trust to get their input.

Some of these lies can be extremely powerful and ingrained in our minds. You may need the help of others to assist you in sorting through them. But do not leave them unattended. It is time to take a hammer at them and eradicate these cancers from your life. You deserve to know the truth.

Core Emotional Triggers
of the Need for Control Child

This is only a partial list, and you may identify additional triggers.
Remember, his emotions occur based on the way he perceives a
current situation. However, his perception of evens may be inccurate.

I feel cheated   I have been victimized
I am in trouble   It is not fair
I feel vulnerable   I am always wrong

What Core Emotional Triggers did you select?

TAKE A MOMENT: Why does your Inner Child use sex to establish control? To prevent bad things from happening or avoid being micromanaged? Describe circumstances you faced that led you to pursue control to reduce your anxiety.

CHAPTER 9
Reason 6: The Entitled-Spiteful Child

"You play the victim so well; I'm surprised you don't carry around your body chalk."

– Author Unknown

"I remember when I was 10, I played on a Little League team, and I hit a home run in our last at-bat to win the game," said Sol, who has battled with pornography since he was 14 and, as an adult has escalated to random sexual encounters using dating apps. *"My parents were not at the game — they never attended. When I got home, they were sitting around the dining room table with some neighbors,*  *and I rushed into the room and announced what I had done.*

"The reaction I received from my parents was faint smiles and my dad uttering, 'That's nice.' The neighbors were extremely excited and heaped me with praise, but it didn't matter because my parents' reaction crushed me. I don't know why it was the norm in my house."

Now 47 and married with one child, Sol still struggles when he senses his wife is unappreciative of his efforts, which he views as disrespectful. He also gets annoyed easily and often when she uses what he refers to as *"the voice."*

"When she takes that condescending tone with me and 'the voice' comes out, I immediately want to run into my office and look at pornography or get on an app and hook up with someone," he said during a session where we discussed resentments. "It's as though I deserve it for how she treats me. When this happens, there is a part of me that does not care if she finds out. It just doesn't matter any longer."

I DO NOT CARE

Of the 12 reasons why men abuse sex, a sense of entitlement is one of the most destructive. As Sol pointed out, with entitlement comes apathy, and men develop an *"I do not care"* attitude about their sexual behavior and how it could negatively impact others. This becomes a slippery slope that finds men justifying their inappropriate sexual behaviors.

"LIFE'S NOT FAIR; WHY SHOULD I BE?"

"Before I started my recovery work and learned how my Inner Child reacts to various emotional triggers, I would be soaking in entitlement if I felt someone was unfair to me," said Asher, whose pornography addiction came to light when his 13-

year-old daughter found porn images on his unguarded laptop. "It was especially bad at work, where I had a hard ass of a boss who would always find fault with anything I did. I spent a great deal of time masturbating in the men's room. My thinking was, 'If you think I suck at my job, then I will spend less time doing it.'"

For Asher, the consistent criticism he endured from his boss triggered his Inner Child's memories of a mom who also offered little positive reinforcement when he was growing up.

"Sorry, but the only word I can think to use to describe my mom is bitch," he said, followed by a heavy sigh. "She was a hard person. I swear I cannot recall ever seeing her smile. Even if you look at photos, you will notice the grim expression on her face.

"She never believed anything I said and always accused me of things I didn't do," he continued. "I felt I was constantly defending myself, and she never listened. So, whenever she started in on me, I would sneak away and look at pornography. I would think, 'now, this is something for her to get upset about.' And it's been the same way ever since. I get offended, and I run off feeling very spiteful."

As Asher pointed out, acting entitled can be an attempt to passive-aggressively punish others when a man feels unjustly accused, unfairly criticized, overly criticized, or threatened.

Dr. Patrick Carnes, a pioneer in treating sexual addiction, referred to this mindset as eroticized rage. "Achieving parity in this way is one of the most common profiles of eroticized rage. Coincidentally, it is also one of the most common causes for affairs," he says. "In a sense, it parallels what object relations theorists have pointed to when aspects of relationships or sex become objectified so that people can 'complete' themselves. The 'object' becomes the piece that was missing. The result is to end up equal to the other or more likely superior."

THE ENTITLED-SPITEFUL INNER CHILD

This Inner Child was made to feel unappreciated or devalued. His sense of entitlement came from being exposed to circumstances he found unfair. Here is a partial list of events that could lead this Inner Child to become activated:

- Falsely accused of things he did not do
- Not being believed when telling the truth
- Being humiliated
- Being criticized
- Not given a voice to express his thoughts or emotions
- Being bullied
- Feeling threatened
- Feeling cheated

As a child or teenager, you had a chip on your shoulders and always looked at what could have or should have been instead of accepting what reality offered. It was not unusual to feel like you always got the short end of the stick. You were the last one picked. It felt like no one wanted to hear what you had to say. You may have been bullied or outcasted. Efforts to connect with others were not received well or met with a lack of interest. Injustice ruled your world.

The experience of being slighted, accused, or rejected would lead to emotions ranging from self-pity to defiance. Your worldview became *"life's not fair."*

After your initial exposure to sex, you learned to use it as a "reward" against the "mistreatment" suffered at the hands of others. Today, as an adult, when a core emotional trigger appears that gives the impression things are not going your way, the Inner Child will be activated and lead the way toward engaging in destructive sexual behaviors. The new worldview has become *"I deserve this."*

As a bonus, this Inner Child also realized that sex allowed him to escape injustice and provided an intense euphoric rush. He understands the sexual activity he is going to engage in will result in a pleasurable sensation that will offset any sense of offense he may be experiencing. Along with this could be the mental and emotional benefits of knowing you have gotten away with something forbidden.

IT IS WHAT MEN DO

Another form of entitlement is expressed by men who believe they do not have to answer to anyone about their behavior. All should accept whatever they deem appropriate, with no questions asked.

"I don't see what the big fuss is about pornography," said Ralph, whose wife threatened to divorce him if he did not seek help. "All men do it. My father did it. My uncles and cousins did it. I knew lots of guys in college who watched it constantly. I think everyone, including my wife, is making a big deal out of this. I don't understand why I can't watch porn if I don't see anything wrong with it."

Men like Ralph do not give a flip to what anyone else thinks or says. They are so inwardly focused and angry they have decided to live among us, abiding by only one set of rules — theirs. It is their world, and we should be happy they are kind enough to share it with us.

> **SOME MEN ARE SO INWARDLY FOCUSED AND ANGRY THEY HAVE DECIDED TO LIVE AMONG US, ABIDING BY ONLY ONE SET OF RULES – THEIRS**

But with this attitude comes a lot of pain — and it is usually not the men who suffer but instead their spouse or partner.

"I have been fighting with him since I first discovered he watched porn, which was two months into our marriage," said Ralph's wife, Lori. "He keeps coming back with the same argument that he is not hurting anyone, and he's not cheating on me. But he doesn't understand. It feels like cheating to me. But he doesn't care. But he will when I finally get up the nerve to see a divorce attorney."

Ralph knows Lori does not like his porn habit, but for him, it is just something she needs to deal with because he has no intention of stopping.

"I use it as a stress reducer," said Ralph, who later recalled growing up in an abusive home. "She's the one who doesn't understand. I need porn to cope with my job, life, and her. I love her and would never have sex with another woman. I don't know what else she wants from me. But I'm not stopping my porn."

Ralph does not get it. He is so convinced Lori is trying to tell him what to do that he cannot recognize her pain. His entitlement trumps her desire for a husband with only eyes for her. In later sessions, when discussing his family of origin, he told the story of living with an abusive older brother who bullied him for years.

"He was a terror," Ralph recalled. "I would have to do his chores and wait on him hand and foot or suffer a beating. I remember telling my dad about it once, and he told me to fight back. My brother was five years older and 45 pounds bigger than me. There was no way to fight back.

"I just learned to go along with what he wanted," he continued. "I couldn't wait for him to leave for college, and when he was gone, I developed the mindset that no one would tell me what to do. And I feel the same way today."

As you listen to Ralph's story, you can sense the depth of his emotional pain and how his Inner Child is hell-bent on never experiencing that again. But he has taken it to the extreme, and his desire to protect himself compromises his ability to see others' distress. If Ralph elects to do his trauma work and process the emotional turmoil endured at the hands of his brother, one day, he will learn how to manage his Inner Child and see how blind he is to the needs and desires of his wife, Lori.

Look What I Did!

Another emotional thrill the Entitled-Spiteful Child receives is the secret knowledge that he has gotten away with something forbidden. It is empowering to know you have invalidated your parents' authority by engaging in activities they would disapprove of.

"Food was always something in my home that my stepfather heavily regulated," said Victor, who had spent thousands of dollars feeding his PSBs (no pun intended). "He would limit the amount we ate while he stuffed his face. My siblings and mother would be hungry, but he did not care. He was satisfied, and that was all that mattered.

"We had a freezer in the basement," he continued. "And I would sneak into the freezer and eat frozen desserts he accumulated. He would buy so much that he never knew I took any. I now know that was the learning ground that taught me how to be a deceitful adult."

As you continue to read, I hope you realize your childhood behaviors were much like Victor's and were developed to assist you in mentally escaping for a brief time from the emotional tension you experienced. These coping strategies distract you from thinking about people and circumstances that cause anxiousness. However, they no longer work for your benefit. To heal, you must remove these unhelpful coping strategies from your life. And how do you do that? You learn to manage your Inner Child.

KID TALK

The Entitled-Spiteful Child is a tough cookie. He is the Child with an attitude, and his ability to rebel makes him extremely challenging. So, what actions can you take to nurture this Inner Child? Here are a few ideas.

You start with education. Your Child needs to understand while he is still emotionally trapped in the times of injustice you faced in the past, today is a new era. Even if you are still experiencing some injustice in your life, the Child must understand healthy ways of dealing with it. His *"I don't care what others think or want"* approach no longer works. It just makes things worse. So, you want to inform him that while you understand his pain, you are taking control and will rationally sort through all difficult circumstances.

You want him to feel your confidence in managing trying situations, which will create a sense of comfort for him. Let him know you can run the show, and he can sit back and watch you work. He is not used to an adult being there to help him deal with emotional discomfort. You are now changing that mindset.

Become proactive in working to reduce your anxiety. It is important to know an increase in anxiety leads to an increase in compulsiveness. And an increase in compulsiveness leads to a higher risk of poor decision-making. Therefore, does it not make sense to work on keeping your anxiety in check? This should be a daily process that includes techniques such as meditation, quiet time, time with God or your higher power, breathing exercises, yoga, physical exercising, and engaging in imagery exercises, to name a few. Keep your anxiety low to better manage your PSBs.

You need to process some of the Child's anger. The resentments he is experiencing have been sitting there far too long. It is time to lance the boils and let the infected wounds drain.

Review the most unjust events you experienced that made you feel mistreated. Discuss those times with your Inner Child and share your sense of pain. Let him know he is not alone and that you understand how he feels. It will bring him great comfort to know someone cares and is looking out for him — maybe for the first time.

If entitlement is one of the reasons you identify with, it is critical to begin sorting through the anger and anxiety linked to your entitlement emotions. You owe it to yourself and those who love you to find real peace in your life.

Core Emotional Triggers of the Entitled-Spiteful Inner Child

This is only a partial list, and you may identify additional triggers. Remember, his emotions occur based on the way he perceives a current situation. However, his perception of events may be inaccurate.

I feel cheated	I feel dismissed
I feel overlooked	I feel falsely accused
Life is not fair	I am not respected
I have no voice	I feel threatened

What Core Emotional Triggers did you select?

TAKE A MOMENT: Does your Inner Child express a need for entitlement? If so, what do you believe occurred in your life that led him to develop his destructive coping mechanism? What resentments are you continuing to hold onto in your life? Who are they aimed at, and why are they so strong?

CHAPTER 10
Reason 7: The Inferior-Weak Child

"When an individual is kept in a situation of inferiority, the fact is he does become inferior."

– Simone de Beauvoir, AUTHOR

Ricky wants to use men for his sexual pleasure. And while he believes he does it out of sexual desire, this behavior is based on his unconscious internal anger toward men. After months of counseling work, Ricky suddenly recalled being sexually abused for nearly a year by an older boy when he was 10.

It was a time in his life that Ricky worked hard to forget. While the memories were not conscious, the emotional pain felt by his Inner Child negatively impacted Ricky's behavior.

"I cannot believe I had forgotten what he did to me. It's not like I was 4," Ricky mumbled with his hands covering his face as he wept. "Why did he do that to me? I just wanted to play with him and have fun. But he made me do degrading things. And I allowed it to happen repeatedly because I was afraid!"

And that is the part that troubles Ricky most. He feels he should have been able to stop this boy, who was six years older, from abusing him sexually, physically, mentally, and emotionally. Giving in to the boy's threats, Ricky endured numerous atrocities at his tormentor's hands, including anal penetration, leaving him feeling shameful and weak.

"I already struggled with inferiority because I was small compared to other boys," he recalled as he stared at the ceiling, trying to avoid eye contact. "And what he did just strengthened that belief I had about myself. I felt puny, and I also felt furious."

As a gay man, Ricky's Inner Child deals with the shame and guilt of being abused, driving Ricky to dominate and control other men to compensate for his weakness and inferiority. His Inner Child was ensuring Ricky would never submit to anyone else by putting him in a position of control over others. This also provided an unhealthy outlet for Ricky to release his anger that had manifested for years.

"After I graduated high school, I changed my attitude and appearance. I gained 25 pounds of muscle and developed a cockiness about myself," he said as he outlined his transformation. "I was determined not to take s--- from anyone. I searched out guys who wanted to be dominated and learned how to take my aggression out on them."

You Are Not Weak Because Your Heart Feels So Heavy

Unknown to Ricky, his Inner Child would be activated whenever he experienced core emotional triggers such as *"I'm powerless"* or *"I feel I don't have a choice."* When activated, his Inner Child had Ricky running off to schedule time with one of his submissive contacts.

"I look back at how I was treating those guys, and I can see how I was simply reenacting what happened to me, but this time, I was the abuser," Ricky said toward the end of our work together. "It's freeing to know I don't have to continue to live that lifestyle any longer and that I can look to establish a normal relationship one day."

Reinforcing Inferiority

Not all men who use sex to feel empowered or reinforce their sense of weakness were sexually abused. Some endured bullying or had parents who programmed them to feel inferior.

"My stepfather was always putting me down and telling me how I disgusted him because I hated athletics and was a bookworm," said Alex, a married, 41-year-old accountant who struggled with same-sex attraction throughout his 18-year marriage.

"I was very unpopular throughout school, especially with other boys," he said. "I was overweight and bullied a great deal. Often, I was ganged up by boys and beaten or humiliated. I always felt like a loser."

Whether physical, emotional, mental, or sexual, horrific actions can lead young boys and teens to believe they are weak and powerless compared to their peers. And in some cases, they discover that through sex, they can reinforce this sense of inferiority.

"It started in college when I would seek out men who were powerful and looking for anonymous sexual encounters," Alex recalled. "I am always the submissive one who serviced the men I met. Rarely does anyone provide me with sexual gratification. But that is okay. I am happy they allow me to spend time with them.

"However, I know I am not gay. I love my wife and enjoy having sex with her, but I get charged up by submitting to men. And I cannot get that sense of arousal with my wife."

After much work together, Alex understood the arousal he experienced from being with other men was not sex-driven but intimacy-related. The encounters made him feel accepted and desired by these men, which he had never experienced with his stepfather. Unfortunately, this acceptance was pseudo and based strictly on Alex's ability to provide sexual gratification to the men he met.

"Understanding why I was pursuing gay sex has changed my life," Alex commented as we started to wind down our counseling relationship. "I still have the urge when I see a well-built man, but with my insight regarding why I want him to notice me, I do not pursue potential opportunities.

"The two men's groups I belong to provide me with a great deal of real acceptance," he continued. "And my improved relationship with God, who I now understand accepts me unconditionally, fills my acceptance cup."

SEX AS POWER

Some men who grow up with insecurities surrounding their manhood fantasize about engaging in sex as the dominant force. An easy outlet to achieve this emotional desire is watching pornography. Through porn, you can experience women and men engaging in any sexual position or activity you desire. You do not have to concern yourself with their orgasm or your performance but solely focus on them being a source of pleasure for you.

Unfortunately, we are seeing an escalation of aggression and physical violence taking place in the pornography world. Just listen to this porn producer describe what men seek regarding pornography. *"People want more violence. Make it harder, make it nastier, make it more relentless."*

THESE MEN USE SEX TO FEEL EMPOWERED OR TO REINFORCE THEIR SENSE OF INFERIORITY

In an edition of the publication, The Guardian, a former porn star who called herself Lisa Ann explained the increased violence in the industry. *"There were times on set with people where I was like, 'This is not a good situation. This is not safe. This girl is out of her mind, and we're not sure what she's going to say when she leaves here.' Everyone is a ticking time bomb, and a lot of it is linked to drugs. Much of this pain comes from these new girls who have to do these abusive scenes because that breaks you down as a woman."*

Clay Olsen is co-founder and CEO of Fight the New Drug. This organization exists to allow individuals to make an informed decision regarding pornography by raising awareness of its harmful effects using science, facts, and personal accounts. As part of its work, the organization keeps track of trends in pornography, and Olsen would agree violence is becoming more prevalent.

"This material is more aggressive, more harmful, more violent, more degrading and damaging than any other time in the history of the world," he reports. "And this generation growing up is dealing with it to an intensity and scale no other generation in the history of the world has ever had to."

Porn is men's consistent outlet to make them feel more empowered and manly. Unfortunately, it is always at the expense of someone else. When men act out with sex to empower themselves, someone will be victimized, used, exploited, manipulated, and have their brokenness taken advantage.

Whether it be porn or engaging with other people in sexual activities, this world of self-indulgence makes these men feel alive. Other people become objects to be used and discarded. In this world, the Inner Child is no longer fearful but powerful.

"In order to feel aroused, we temporarily transform ourselves from frogs into princes," wrote Michael Bader in his book

Arousal. "Sexual fantasies undo rejections, turn helplessness into power, redeem feelings of unworthiness, and stamp out even the slimmest vestiges of depression. For just a few moments, just long enough to have an orgasm, the Walter Mitty in all of us – the ordinary person with dreams of grandeur – imagines himself to be sexually powerful."

Yep, this guy is using sex to feel powerful and forceful. But again, it is just pseudo. His feelings of inadequacy still exist and serve to frighten and activate his Inner Child repeatedly.

SEX REINFORCING INFERIORITY

After confessing to his wife, Benny called me to say he had been cruising ads on Craig's List seeking gay sex. He reported never having a sexual encounter with another man but often watched gay porn. Benny believed he was straight but had some reservations and wanted clarity.

"I really can't imagine having sex with a man; however, on my last road trip, I did answer an ad and invited a man to my hotel room," he said in a low whisper. "But I didn't answer the door. I was afraid. It was at that point I knew I needed help."

IT IS NOT UNCOMMON FOR INDIVIDUALS WHO HAVE SUFFERED TRAUMA TO REENACT THEIR TRAUMA

Over the following weeks, Benny told the story of growing up in a home with two siblings – in which he was the middle child surrounded by two sisters. He shared that his relationship with his dad was distant, and for some reason, his father never took an interest in him. However, his father was engaged and active in his siblings' lives. Benny also recalled being a timid and quiet boy who had difficulty making friends at school or in the neighborhood.

"For some reason, no one wanted to be my friend," he told me. "So many kids in elementary school bullied me, and I would always try and find a space where I could be alone. I would not exaggerate if I told you I didn't have a single friend until I was a junior in high school, and then I got to hang out with a couple of my younger sister's friends.

"But growing up, for some reason, girls were not interested in me, and boys hated me," he continued with a profound sense of sadness etched on his face. "It was a difficult childhood."

Benny often questioned himself, wondering, *"what's wrong with me."* He could not understand how boys would not want to be his friend. Add to that a father who showed no interest in his son, and you have the making of a confused child.

Until one day, his father suddenly expressed an interest in spending time with him. When Benny was nine, his father approached him one morning and said, *"hey, you need to get washed; let's go hit the shower."* And that is what they did. For the next year, Benny showered with his father nearly every morning.

"Nothing sexual happened," Benny said, eager to remove any concerning ideas he thought I might be formulating. "At least, I don't recall. I found it both exciting and strange. I was thrilled my dad was spending time with me but being naked and close to him in a very tight area was weird."

BENNY'S INNER CHILD

So, let us summarize. Benny grows up being rejected by all males, including the most influential in his life – his dad. But at some point, his father demonstrates an interest in spending time with him, but in a way that has sexual overtones. Can you smell confusion for a young boy in those circumstances?

Like Alex, Benny's Inner Child believes he is different (inferior) from other males, so they shun him. Meanwhile, his Inner Child received an indirect message from his father, saying, *"men will be your friend if you are sexual with them."*

Benny struggles most when his Inner Child experiences core emotional triggers such as *"he does not like me"* or *"I don't fit in."* In therapy, Benny identified these, and other core emotional triggers delivered by negative events in his daily life. Benny may be unaware of these core emotional triggers when they hit, but his Inner Child notices them immediately. When that happens, the Child is off to seek comfort – by distracting himself from the hurtful core emotional triggers. And the activities he normally selects are usually destructive.

In Benny's case, that comfort came through attempts to be validated and accepted by other men. But his Inner Child believed this could only be accomplished by being sexual with men.

For a long time, gay porn successfully served that role allowing Benny to gain a sense of affirmation through fantasy. But over time, fantasy did not generate the dopamine rush required to give Benny a sense of acceptance. That is when he turned to Craig's List to ramp up the intensity level.

> ## THIS INNER CHILD EXPERIENCES CORE EMOTIONAL TRIGGERS SUCH AS *"THEY THINK I'M WEAK"* OR *"I DON'T FIT IN"*

"I know in my heart I don't want to have sex with men," he explained. "But I do want to have male friends. Something in me kept saying that the only way possible was to give myself to men sexually. But the thought of actually doing that troubled me."

After much challenging work in therapy, Benny's Inner Child still gets upset when something occurs that brings on a core emotional trigger. However, Benny now has the insights and skills needed to help soothe the Child and avoid seeking an escape from the negative emotions being experienced.

"I have been very successful in using the What I Feel Versus What is Real method you taught me," said Benny about a key component of the Inner Child Model™, which he went on to explain. "When I start to experience core emotional triggers, I slow everything down, and I sit with them, allowing myself to feel the hurt I experienced when I was younger. After processing the emotional discomfort, I continue to slow things down by shifting my thinking to what is real. While I may feel a male co-worker has ignored me, I use my wise mind to explain to my Inner Child the co-worker probably has something else on his mind and is too distracted to notice me. But he is not intentionally blowing me off. I know he thinks well of me as a co-worker."

WHAT IS REAL?

Utilizing the *What I Feel Versus What is Real* component of the Inner Child Model™ is critical in helping men like Benny manage their Inner Children and learn to stay one step ahead of the PSBs. In slowing down your reaction to core emotional triggers, you stall your compulsiveness, which plays a significant role in your addictive behaviors.

Think of this as a speed bump. If you maintain the same rate of speed without slowing down as you approach a speed bump, at best, you endure a violent jolt. At worst, you end up causing severe damage to your car's front end. That is the consequence of not slowing down.

As you have discovered, there were tremendous aftermaths regarding engaging in your PSBs. Imagine slowing everything down and thinking through your pending actions before jumping off the cliff. Life may be much more peaceful for you and your loved ones.

Taking the time and processing your core emotional triggers before they send your Inner Child into a hissy fit can be accomplished by utilizing the *What I Feel Versus What is Real* component of this model. But more about this later. But now, back to the Inferior-Weak Child.

OBJECTIFICATION

Porn promotes the objectification of others, and for men who believe they are inferior and weak, objectification is essential to their excitement and fulfillment.

In many cases, a man who correlates a sense of inferiority with his sexuality will see sex as impersonal and merely a vehicle to achieve the emotional satisfaction of being empowered or humiliated. Again, in his book, *Arousal: The Secret Logic of Sexual Fantasies,* Dr. Bader describes the role of objectification this way.

"Sexual objectification – the experience of another person as if he or she were only a body or a part of a body – is employed by men in the interest of achieving psychological safety," he writes. "Like ruthlessness, objectification momentarily eliminates a woman's emotional life, a life for which men expect to feel responsible and with which they will feel drawn to identify. If they are connecting only with a body and not a whole person, then they can 'use' that body without worrying about the emotional consequences. A body isn't sad or hurt, doesn't have needs, or makes demands, and isn't a cauldron of feelings with which the man might identify and, as a result, lose his boundaries and masculinity."

It sounds very cold because it is.

The brokenness experienced by men like Alex and Benny leads to engaging in sexual activities most people would never consider. And much of this activity is based on power or its perceived lack.

Some yield their power to reinforce their sense of inferiority, while others take power to mask their feelings of weakness. Either way, it is all directed by a confused Inner Child.

OTHER COPING STRATEGIES

Not all men who resonate with the Inferior-Weak Child will use sex as a coping strategy to escape their emotional anguish. Many become conflict-avoidant and struggle not to be defensive or to stay present during trying circumstances.

"I hate conflict," said Wilder, whose passive demeanor screams of someone who deals with many fears. "I am the ultimate people-pleaser, but that leaves me very anxious that I may not achieve what I set out to do for others, leaving them disappointed and angry with me."

Wilder is a 28-year-old computer analyst who has only been married for 10 months and recently confessed to his wife that he had been using an Internet sex chat game to communicate with numerous women before the start of their relationship.

"As you know, she is dealing with betrayal trauma — which I still don't believe I fully understand — and I am having difficulty dealing with her anger," he explained. "I keep trying to find ways to make her happy, but nothing is working. It has me in a constant state of anxiety.

"I find myself doing what I have always done when there is conflict, I shut down," he continued. "And my wife is telling me that is making everything worse. But I don't know what to do."

Other men who can relate to the Inferior-Weak Child have learned to isolate themselves from others and activities they believe may make them look foolish.

"I love baseball," said Hank, age 51, whose wife left him 6-months ago because of his passion for prostitutes. "For years, I wanted to play on the company softball team, but I have not because I was afraid I would make a fool of myself. That has been a problem all my life. I never take chances, and I know I missed out a lot. I think that may be part of the reason I went to prostitutes, to experience something different than my normal life."

Hank's defense mechanism to deal with his core emotional triggers, *"I am not good enough"* and *"I am a failure"* is to keep a low profile and engage as little as possible. His Inner Child believes this keeps him secure, but in reality, it only exacerbates his emotions of being seen as inferior and weak.

KID TALK

As you have been learning, empowerment comes when you take back control from the Inner Child and apply rational thinking to your circumstances. Here are steps to deal with the Inferior-Weak Child and empower yourself.

- Like the other Inner Children we have discussed, this little guy has gone through many emotional and mental distresses. A large part of his problem is he is confused about what it means to be a man. All he knows is he does not feel like one. Therefore, part of your responsibility is to educate him on the virtues of a real man. And this includes the fact that sometimes it is ok for a man to feel fearful.

- When he becomes triggered, your Inner Child needs to know the current circumstance that brings him emotional distress is something you can effectively manage. He needs to understand the inferiority he feels is something you can rationalize and look at from a different perspective. As you learn his pain points, your responsibility turns toward soothing him by demonstrating your ability to manage the current situation.

Core Emotional Triggers of the Inferior-Weak Inner Child

This is only a partial list, and you may identify additional triggers. Remember, his emotions occur based on the way he perceives a current situation. However, his perception of evens may be inccurate.

I am useless	I am weak
I am a fraud	I am a loser
I am powerless	I do not matter
I am insignificant	I am a mistake

What Core Emotional Triggers did you select?

_____

TAKE A MOMENT: What were the events/people who led your Inner Child to feel inferior and weak? How did they do this? What core emotional triggers do you believe activate your Inner Child?

_____

Bonus Exercise:

Commit to practicing **What I Feel Versus What is Real** for 5 days. Please note you can use this technique in any circumstance that causes you to experience emotional distress. I have clients who practice this daily. Record each time you utilize this slowing-down technique by answering the following questions. Later, share the results with your therapist/coach.

- What was the negative event that activated one of your Core Emotional Triggers?
- What Core Emotional Trigger(s) did you experience?
- What was it like to sit and process the emotional discomfort? Be detailed.
- What Wise Mind rationales did you use to explain the REAL situation to your Inner Child?
- What actions did you take after using this approach?

CHAPTER 11

Reason 8: The Stressed Child

"We must have a pie. Stress cannot exist in the presence of a pie."

– David Mamet, Author

Liam has a tough time differentiating his emotions from those experienced by his wife. He often finds himself working hard to ensure she remains in a good mood, and if that should change, he fanatically works to repair the situation to revert her into a positive state of mind.

When Liam finds himself unsuccessful in managing her mood – which he often is – he begins to crash emotionally and considers himself a  failure and a lousy husband. Attempting to manage the emotional state of others can be highly exhausting, as Liam knows, which is why he often engages in porno and masturbation to reduce his anxiety.

"I started looking at porn when I was 11 or 12," the 29-year-old public relations executive recalled. "My home life was difficult. There was no trauma, but Mom and Dad didn't see eye-to-eye, and Dad made sure to stay out of the house often. That left me alone, listening to Mom complain about how sad and hurt she was by my absent father. She would lay on her bed, crying, and I would hold her trying to make it better. Porn was my way of leaving the heaviness behind in caring for her."

Liam described what we refer to as emotional incest – a form of enmeshment – where a parent leans heavily on a child for emotional support and comfort. For these children, their emotions take a back seat to their parents' emotions, and the objective is to maintain stability. It is an awkward position for a child to be placed. (You will read more about this topic when we review the Enmeshed Child in Chapter 13.)

"I remember as a teenager, I would tell her I was going out with friends, and without fail, just before my leaving, she would develop some type of illness or injury," he said as I watched him nervously fidgeting with his fingers and hands. "I would feel guilty and end up killing my plans and spending the night watching television or talking with her. And, of course, her illness or injury would always clear up.

PORN IS A SHORT-TERM FIX TO MANAGING ANXIETY BECAUSE OF THE UNWANTED CONSEQUENCES THAT FOLLOW

"This started when I was eight, and it left me always feeling like I was walking on eggshells," he continued with his hands still nervously wiggling. "I have always been anxious, and I use pornography to distract myself from my nervousness."

Men like Liam grew up feeling anxious due to experiencing neglect, abuse, or traumatic events at home or elsewhere. At some point, they discover sex and realize it soothes their anxiety by serving as a distraction (although, as children and teens, they probably do not realize it is being utilized as a distraction).

However, once they are finished, the anxiety reappears, causing them to rely more heavily on sexual activities to lessen their stress levels. This is why some young boys, teens, and men masturbate numerous times daily. There is no doubt pornography can reduce anxiety by stimulating the body and mind as a man becomes sexually aroused. And since many men masturbate when looking at porn, orgasm leads to a state of relaxation.

However, it is all a short-term fix, as chronic porn usage nearly always leads to unwanted consequences. These could include guilt and shame, relational distress, wasted time, isolation, sexual dysfunction issues, obsessions with sexual thoughts, fantasies, distorted views of sex, work or legal issues, and escalation to other PSBs.

Over time, the continued use of pornography has little to do with a man's obsession with sex and more with a need to release his stress and anxiety. In fact, some men struggling with PSBs may soon find they cannot manage their stress in any manner other than utilizing sex for soothing.

You Mean to Tell Me a Stress Ball Isn't for Throwing at People Who Stress You Out?

Liam's Inner Child

Liam recognizes the anxiousness caused by his mom, but he has never identified and dealt with the core emotional triggers that activate his Inner Child. For Liam, his Inner Child starts to panic and seeks comfort with porn when the following core emotional triggers strike: *"Things are out of control," "I'm helpless," "I'm afraid,"* or *"I lack confidence."* All the core emotional triggers that activate Liam's Inner Child are related to emotions he often experienced when serving as an emotional surrogate for his mother.

"I worked so hard to keep things under control at home with Mom," he explained while pointing out feelings of helplessness are the worst. "During the times when nothing I did worked to snap her out of her depressed mood were the most stressful. I was scared she would act on her threat to kill herself. All I could think about was my father would blame me if anything happened to her."

Fear is a significant activator for Liam's Inner Child, with many being irrational and leading him to worry about things he cannot control — like his mother's threats of suicide, where Liam felt responsible for keeping her alive.

"I'm a big-time worrier, and it drives my wife crazy," he said, slowly shaking his head. "While getting rid of my porn problem is my first goal, learning not to worry all the time is second."

As Liam does his recovery work and drills more deeply into the negative impact his mother's emotional incest had on him, he should find himself experiencing less worry and being more at peace. And the key will be in confronting and rationalizing with his frightened Inner Child.

STRESS AND PSBS

Over the years, researchers have discovered a strong correlation between stress and addictive behaviors. An article by Dr. Shahram Heshmat entitled *Stress and Addiction: Chronic Stress Can Increase Vulnerability to Addiction* points out this issue is more likely to occur in individuals who dealt with high stress as children.

"There is solid evidence for the link between chronic stress and the motivation to use addictive substances." writes Dr. Heshmat in the May 2017 edition of Psychology Today Magazine. *"Research shows adverse childhood experiences such as physical and sexual abuse, neglect, domestic violence, and family dysfunction are associated with an increased risk of addiction. The experience of childhood abuse and neglect indirectly increases the risk of addiction through decreased self-control."*

Those who struggle with stress also are more likely to have trouble dealing with compulsive behaviors. Numerous studies have demonstrated that high stress levels result in individuals' inability to delay gratification. This action is partly because chronic stress negatively impacts various brain areas, including the prefrontal lobe, which is responsible for motivation, executive thinking, and impulse control. It is also believed that stress negatively impacts the brain's reward center, which can exacerbate cravings.

The Adverse Childhood Experiences (ACE) Study – conducted by the CDC and Kaiser-Permanente – demonstrated that children who deal with stress due to abuse or neglect have a dramatically higher risk of developing addictive behaviors as they age. For these individuals, addictive activities are often utilized to help cope with stress and anxiety.

The equation below clearly explains stress's impact on developing addictive behaviors such as PSBs.

STRESS = ANXIETY = COMPULSIVENESS = BAD DECISION MAKING

As you can see, to effectively deal with PSBs, your stress level must be proactively managed. This requires developing a game plan that will enable you to focus on reducing your stress daily. Please note this is not a suggestion. Working to lower your stress must be part of your everyday recovery program.

Controlling your compulsiveness will not only assist you in dealing with your PSBs but also help you to assist your partner in healing from your betrayal. It also can help you in other areas of your life, including anger management, eating disorders, mood management, productivity, motivation, etc.

I would encourage you to put this book down and take time to develop a plan to manage your stress. One of the best techniques is to do daily motivation. You can find more information, including a gift, at the end of this chapter. Please take advantage of this; it can change EVERYTHING.

HIDDEN ANXIETY

Some men raised in abusive or neglectful environments learned at an early age how to suppress their anxiety by keeping a low profile, not sharing information, and staying busy. They learned to desensitize their anxiety – and some reached a point where they could not feel it. One way they accomplished this was by running, running, and running.

"I'm not the anxious type, but I can't slow down," says Tony, a lifelong bachelor and master gardener who owns a landscaping business. He also has an expensive habit of engaging with escorts. *"I get about four hours of sleep a night, and I go from the time I get up until I crash at night. It's just my speed – go, go, go."*

As Tony and I talked, I discussed the possibility of him sitting quietly for two to three minutes. As I suggested this simple exercise, his facial expression changed to one of shock. *"I cannot do that,"* he said in a serious but monotone voice. *"I cannot do that."*

I knew then Tony had been suppressing his anxiety for decades. He was an extremely stressful person, but somewhere along the line, he buried emotions and convinced himself he was unshakeable. Nothing could be further from the truth, and his go-go-go lifestyle and constant desire for escorts proved the point. He cannot feel his anxiety because he uses busyness (a coping strategy) to keep it at bay.

Starting at an early age, Tony used a non-stop schedule and sex as distractions to manage the anxiety he experienced in his home growing up. Raised by his father – after his mom died when Tony was seven – he watched his dad struggle to move on. Although there was no abuse in the home, which consisted of only Tony and his father, there was little else. Tony's dad suffered from depression and struggled to get out of bed some days. As a young boy, Tony went from having a mother who met his needs to no one being available.

He learned to become very self-efficient, not imposing upon his father. Still, he worried a great deal about making innocent mistakes for fear of placing additional burdens on his already troubled dad.

"After mom died, the house died," Tony explained, who looked years older than his age 44. "There was no life in it. My dad and I were existing, not living. But I worried about him all the time. He was all I had left in the world. Do you know what it is like trying to cook your food and hoping you do not start a fire or make a mess? It was not that I feared getting in trouble; I was afraid of adding any additional stress to my dad's life."

So, Tony took on that stress, which was a lot for a young boy. To help cope with his fearful emotions, he became active both in and outside the home. He cleaned, cooked, and kept things quiet at home while participating in baseball and basketball.

"I needed to stay busy, so I didn't think about losing my dad," he said as he continued to do excellent work in therapy, gaining the valuable insights needed to protect his Inner Child and eliminate his dependency on escorts. *"I learned that keeping active kept my mind off my worries and fears. And it worked."*

As a child, staying busy was not Tony's only way of keeping an active mind. He also discovered how sex could be a distraction to soothe his anxiety. He would spend hours looking at the lingerie photos in a Sears catalog and later was introduced to pornography by friends in the neighborhood. As a young adult, he later escalated to engaging with prostitutes.

TONY'S INNER CHILD

As we continued our work, Tony discovered his Inner Child struggled when one of the following core emotional triggers appeared: *"I'm uncomfortable," "I can't make a mistake," "I feel trapped,"* or *"I feel alone."* Tony understood he never properly grieved the death of his mother because he immediately turned his focus on the fear of losing his dad.

We also discovered he repressed anger and feelings of abandonment by his mom, whose death left Tony alone to deal with a depressed father. For Tony's Inner Child, prostitutes served as a source of female nurturing and provided security by not allowing him to get emotionally involved. He realized he never married because of the irrational fear of losing his spouse.

As he continued his recovery work, Tony started to experience more anxious emotions that he had attempted to keep hidden. And the more he connected with his feelings and Inner Child, the more he slowed down his schedule. He also stopped frequenting escorts and later started dating.

"I never realized how much stress I was dealing with," he said toward the end of our work together. "Now that I have faced my stress and my Inner Child, I see very clearly all of the defenses he put in place to keep me from feeling. Looking back, it was all crazy. I'm glad I have come to know my Inner Child, but he's a handful."

KID TALK

Besides being there for your Inner Child emotionally, one of the most effective ways to assist him is learning to have fun. That is right. Enjoy yourself. Enjoy others. Enjoy life. This Child lives to escape and has spent his life doing it with unhealthy behaviors. Show him there can be a healthy and fun balance in life.

This is part of an overall self-care program that is critical for recovery and vital for the Inner Child who experiences chronic anxiety. Learn to be silly, even if you do so in private. But taking risks and trying to be humorous and adventurous with others would be much better.

Growing up in a tense environment leaves this kid on the alert, and you need to take him down a notch. He will never cease being vigilant about potential risks, so it is your job to let him know an adult is available to protect him. He does not have to go it alone as he did when you were younger. Tell him you will be the decision-maker when selecting the type of comfort needed to reduce stress.

It's also helpful to understand we cannot control all circumstances that get dropped in our lap. You can do a stellar job taking care of your body and doing the right things to be healthy, but that does not mean you are immune to disease, illnesses, or injuries. You cannot control the inconsiderate and reckless actions of others that may bring discomfort into your life. What you can control is how to deal with these situations. It would be wise to stop worrying about what you cannot control.

Stress is part of our lives. But as men, we do a disservice to ourselves when we attempt to escape our emotions, including fear. You must feel to heal. And feeling includes allowing ourselves to experience negative and hurtful emotions as well as positive ones. As men, the commitment to continuous self-reflection and learning valuable insights about ourselves, our past, and our behaviors should be a never-ending mission. Now, go forth and feel.

Core Emotional Triggers
of the Stressed Inner Child

This is only a partial list, and you may identify additional triggers.
Remember, his emotions occur based on the way he perceives a
current situation. However, his perception of evens may be inccurate.

I feel overwhelmed	I feel out of control
I am going crazy	I feel uncomfortable
Life is too much	I lack confidence
I am incapable	I am helpless

Which Core Emotional Triggers did you select?

TAKE A MOMENT: Can you recall sources of stress and anxiety in your childhood and teen years? Perhaps it occurred at home, school, or among peers. Take a few moments and write about the anxiety you faced growing up. How do you believe it impacts your ability to manage stress today? What core emotional triggers activate this Inner Child for you?

What commitments can you make to manage your stress better?

Take a moment and read this article to get some ideas on how to manage stress: www.sexuallypuremen.com/2023/05/07/10-ways-to-manage-stress/

Also, use the link below to obtain a free library of meditation music. It has generously been provided by a colleague of mine, Bill Herr, LCSW, CSAT.

Commit to meditating for 10 minutes a day. Focus on the music and your breathing. If intrusive thoughts appear – and they will – turn your attention back to the music and/or your breathing. The objective is to learn to be still and allow your body and mind to experience relaxation. Be sure to breathe gently throughout your meditation sessions. I promise if you stick with it, you will see amazing results.

https://www.alternatingsounds.com

CHAPTER 12

Reason 9: The Early Sexually Stimulated and/or Sexually Abused Child

"Dissociation gets you through a brutal experience, letting your basic survival skills operate unimpeded...your ability to survive is enhanced as the ability to feel is diminished. All feelings are blocked – you go away."

– Renee Fredrickson, Author

As he sat across from me, the tears in Arnold's eyes started to form before he could utter his first word. At the end of our last session, he told me he was sexually abused as a child. Arnold had never shared it with anyone, including this wife, and he had waited to determine if I was safe before disclosing his dark, long-kept secret.

Arnold was a 39-year-old married father of three and had led a covert life until three months ago when he was arrested in a public park while engaging in sex with another man. It was common for him to visit places once or twice weekly where men meet for casual sex. But he also had encounters in other men's homes and motels.

After the arrest, his attorney recommended Arnold start counseling to demonstrate his commitment to change to the judge. In therapy, we created a structured routine, developed a support network, and, most importantly, determined why he abused sex.

However, I did not know I was missing an extremely critical piece of information that would change the scope of our therapy and ultimately be a catalyst for Arnold to engage with his Inner Child and facilitate healing.

ARNOLD'S STORY

Arnold was about to lead me through a nightmare. In my wildest imagination, I could never comprehend a child enduring what he experienced at the hands of adults. It started when he was 10. His mother, Sarah, an alcoholic living on welfare, started dating a new guy. New men in the home were not unusual. They came and went through Sarah's bed like a revolving door.

FORGETTING IS DIFFICULT. REMEMBERING IS WORSE.

The men who showed up often ignored Arnold, and he preferred it that way. He lived in his world, spending endless hours watching television in the living room as his mother entertained her "friends." But this guy would permanently scar this young, innocent boy.

Arnold cannot recall the man's name, but he remembers he was around for a good part of six months. He showed up every Friday night with two friends who would hang out, getting high and drunk with Sarah.

The evenings turned into trouble after Sarah passed out – and she would always pass out after partying hard. That is when her new man and his friends would take turns raping and sodomizing Arnold. The man and his friends threatened to kill Arnold's mother if he told her what was happening. Scared of losing his mom, he silently endured their sexual torture. He came to dread Fridays – a feeling he still struggles with today. As the abuse continued, Arnold learned how to dissociate to avoid the pain and humiliation he was enduring. While his body was still suffering the abuse, he was in a special, safe place in his mind.

The abuse ended when the man was sent to prison for selling drugs. But for Arnold, there was no escaping the emotional and mental anguish he endured. He would spend the rest of his youth and early adult life trapped in his hellish prison, including engaging in risky sexual behaviors.

Even though the abuse happened decades ago, Arnold's eroded self-worth and self-loathing led to blaming himself for what happened. That self-loathing drives Arnold to punish himself by engaging in sex where men use him.

"I am ashamed to admit this, but I allow men to hurt me physically," he told me during our first session. "I also hate to admit that I enjoy what they do to me, although some hurt me very badly, including one who broke three of my teeth."

In cases like Arnold's, individuals who have been sexually abused may seek to reenact their abuse. Arnold did this partly because he felt he deserved to continue to be abused because he did nothing to stop the original abuse he endured.

HURTING OTHERS

Individuals who endure sexual abuse develop numerous negative narratives and irrational beliefs about themselves and sex. This can lead a person – such as Arnold – to use sex to inflict pain and suffering upon themselves or to hurt others.

"I was bullied and sexually abused for many years by an older cousin who lived with us," said Cal, who came into counseling after his wife of 21 years discovered he participated in BDSM activities with multiple women.

"He was always hitting me, and if I didn't do what he wanted, he would lock me in a wooden chest. It was terrifying," he recalled with his hands trembling slightly. "He had complete control over me because I didn't want to go back into the box.

"After the abuse stopped when I reached high school, I started fantasizing about dominating others," Cal continued. "But I never acted upon it until I stumbled across bondage chatrooms long after marriage. Over time, I got deeper into the BDSM world and went from viewing bondage porn sites to meeting women who liked that form of sex.

"Once I experienced the power of dominating someone sexually, I was hooked. It was a complete 180 from what my cousin did to me, and for the first time in my life, I felt strong," he said as I watched his head drop. "It's pathetic. I needed to hurt women to feel strong. And worst, it has destroyed my wife, who didn't deserve this."

PORN IS SERVING AS THE PREDOMINANT RESOURCE IN EDUCATING OUR KIDS ABOUT SEX AND RELATIONSHIPS

Sexual abuse of children is a horrific crime that can mentally and emotionally disfigure boys and girls for the rest of their lives. The National Center for Victims of Crimes' (NCVC) statistics show that 1 in 5 girls and 1 in 20 boys are victims of child sexual abuse. The organization also believes this number does not represent the true magnitude of the problem because this crime is often not reported. And experts agree the incidence is far higher than what is disclosed to authorities.

In my practice, 2 out of 10 men report being sexually violated as a child. While this is not a scientific measure, the 20%

population I see is much higher than the 5% population recorded by NCVC.

OTHER EARLY EXPOSURE

Not all men exposed to sex at an early age were sexually abused. Many accidentally stumbled across or were introduced to pornography. Others may have witnessed or heard their parents or others having sex.

Through extensive clinical studies, we know that consistent use of pornography can lead to devastating effects on the human brain, including addictive properties, distorted views of sex, and sexual dysfunction. When exposed at an early age, young minds – which are very impressionable –do not know what to make of the raw images.

When first exposed to pornography, most children are spooked and somewhat repulsed by what they observe. But curiosity usually gets the best of them, and they return for more. The more they watch, the more their negative feelings about porn subside. In fact, the desire to act out what they see increases for a handful of boys.

"A significant minority of children want to emulate what they have seen in online pornography," writes researcher Elena Martellozzo in her paper entitled, A quantitative and qualitative examination of the impact of online pornography on the values, attitudes, beliefs, and behaviors of children and young people. "During our research, we also discovered there is a perception, particularly from boys, that what they have viewed is realistic."

Doesn't that scare the hell out of you – that pornography serves as the predominant resource in educating our kids about sex and relationships? It certainly has me worried. Here is more on the subject.

"Studies suggest that youth who consume pornography may develop unrealistic sexual values and beliefs," writes the late Gary Wilson in his best-selling book Your Brain on Porn. "Among the findings, higher levels of permissive sexual attitudes, sexual preoccupation, and earlier sexual experimentation have been correlated with more frequent consumption of pornography."

The bottom line is pornography shows boys it is okay to objectify girls and teaches girls it is okay to be objectified. That is unbelievable. Worst yet, it is a recipe for creating social and interpersonal disasters for our youth.

In his book, *Treating Pornography Addiction: The Essential Tools for Recovery*, Dr. Kevin Skinner notes boys exposed to sex at an early age may not mature emotionally as well as their peers.

"Because early sexual experiences are so profound to the child's mind, he can become fixated on sexual thoughts and feelings," Skinner writes. "Some researchers suggest that strong negative emotional experiences stunt a person's emotional development and maturity. When emotional development slows, and the mind gets stuck on sexual feelings, a serious sexual addiction is a likely outcome."

Skinner is dead on with his assessment. Most young boys exposed to sex at an early age struggle to become men. They struggle to mature emotionally. I know. I used to be one of them. There are too many boys over the age of 25 running around today. I do not mean to be insulting. It is just reality. We must commit to growing up and becoming the men God designed us to be so that we can engage in authentic relationships. But that is part of the trouble; we have no idea what emotional maturity looks like or how to achieve it.

You can learn much more about emotionally undeveloped men in my book, **Why Men Struggle to Love: Overcoming Relational Blind Spots.**

KID TALK

If you were a victim of sexual abuse, the most helpful thing you can do for your Inner Child is to grieve with him as he experiences emotional triggers that bring back traumatic memories. We are trying to move away from continuing to repress or suppress past emotional wounds. Accomplishing this requires a great deal of courage on your part. If you find yourself struggling, I strongly encourage you to seek the help of a professional specializing in childhood trauma.

Anne Kerr, the former CEO of the True North Freedom Project, encourages individuals to uncover past abuses and heal sexual wounds to move forward healthily with their lives.

"Our sexuality is a central and good aspect of our humanity that leads us to connection and intimacy on many levels," says Anne, whose organization is committed to helping singles, couples, parents, and ministry leaders develop a God-honoring understanding of sexuality. *"It's powerful for*

good but also for evil. Pornography and sexual abuse are counterfeits of true intimacy that can quickly change how we view ourselves, others, the world, and God. Because sexuality is such a significant aspect of our humanity, dealing with early sexual encounters and working to discover healing and redemption for them can also be quite powerful for growth."

Another way to assist your Child is to ensure he no longer blames himself for what occurred. It is not unusual for children who have been sexually abused to feel guilty and ashamed of what happened. In some cases, the abuser will convince the child he was at fault by being suggestive or seductive. Or saying if the child did not like it, he would have done more to stop it from occurring. These are nothing but lies that must be snuffed out.

You must put an end to needless emotional trauma. Use encouraging words and clearly explain to your Inner Child that he is not at fault for what occurred—no more lies. Put the blame where it belongs – on your predator(s).

The impact of the events that occurred has made your life difficult, to say the least. But real healing can be found if you are willing to apply the time and confront the ghosts of the past. You cannot continue to be a victim any longer. It is time to become a survivor. Embrace your Inner Child and let him know he is okay. Let yourself know that you are okay and should not be ashamed.

Core Emotional Triggers of the Early Sexually Stimulated/Abused Inner Child

This is only a partial list, and you may identify additional triggers. Remember, his emotions occur based on the way he perceives a current situation. However, his perception of evens may be inccurate.

I feel dirty/unclean
I feel damaged
I feel worthless

I feel broken
I am broken
I feel defective

Which Core Emotional Triggers did you select?

TAKE A MOMENT: Outline early exposure to sex or sexual materials and/or any sexual abuse you may have suffered. Are you surprised by anything you noted? If you were exposed to sex at an early age or were sexually abused, how do you believe it has impacted your life as an adult?

Do you agree you have not fully emotionally matured? Why do you agree with that statement?

EXTREMELY IMPORTANT
INFORMATION

One question often asked is how likely someone is who was sexually abused as a child to sexually victimize others.

Statistics on this subject vary, but a meta-analysis of empirical studies containing a total of 1,717 subjects found 28% of sex offenders reported a history of childhood sexual abuse, (Hanson & Slater, 1988).

This is significantly greater than the 17% rate outlined by Dr. Mic Hunter in his book *"The Sexually Abused Male."*

The bottom line is a large majority of men who were sexually abused as children do not become pedophiles or sexual predators. The same can be said for men struggling with a PSBs. Only a small segment of them will become sexual offenders.

That being said, the wounds of child sexual abuse should not be ignored. Please seek help if you have been victimized.

CHAPTER 13

Reason 10: The Enmeshed Child

"While we are in a dysfunctional, shame-based relationship, we may feel like we are losing our mind, going crazy. When we try to test reality, we cannot trust our senses, feelings, and reactions."
—Charles L. Whitfield, Author

Imagine you are driving on a six-lane highway that has no lane markings. You and hundreds of other drivers would be forced to navigate the black roadway without guidance or direction from the much-needed white markings. Where one lane starts, and the other ends would be up to each driver.

You would be at the mercy of others to ensure they lined up correctly, forming make-shift lanes for the entire length of the interstate to avoid crossing into another's lane.

I am not sure about you, but that is a highway I would avoid at all costs. This word picture should give you a sense of what it is like to be raised in an enmeshed family system. No boundaries. No limitations. Much anxiety. Lots of crashes. Many, many injuries. In a few words, the environment is toxic.

THE HEALTHY ATTACHMENT

At the heart of all relationships is attachment. But what exactly does attachment mean? An attachment is an emotional bond shared between two or more individuals. For many people, the ability to form attachments is natural and feels rewarding, bringing them stability. Healthy attachments, also known as secure attachments, occur when individuals receive the nurturing and guidance required during the initial stages of childhood development, enabling them to cultivate strong and flourishing bonds. This critical time determines whether a healthy connection between infants and caregivers will be established and also serves as a predictor for developing authentic relationships in the future.

The essential emotional components provided by caregivers during this early development period include the following:

- **Connection** allows individuals to accept and give physical and emotional touch and engage in meaningful relationships with others. These individuals often experience emotions of comfort, safety, and reassurance.

- **Attunement** is when individuals can determine the emotional needs of others. They can read facial expressions and body language that provide them with insights into the emotional needs, wants, and desires of others. Attuned individuals are extremely confident around people.

- **Trust** provides an individual with feelings that others love, protect, and accept him. These individuals feel valued by others and can establish trustworthy relationships.

- **Autonomy** allows individuals to be independent and not intimidated when making decisions. These individuals feel secure.

- **Integration of Love and Sexuality** leads to developing deep, emotional connections. Physical needs do not supersede emotional needs.

This healthy bond makes individuals comfortable engaging in relationships, identifying and expressing their emotions, and being vulnerable. The dedicated efforts of them caregivers increase the odds of these children becoming involved in relationships that ultimately lead to the creation of healthy connections.

THE UNHEALTHY ATTACHMENTS

Numerous research studies estimate between 40-45% of the U.S. population have a secure attachment. But that leaves more than half of the population lacking the foundation to form healthy attachment bonds. This is certainly true of those children raised in enmeshed environments that stifle individualism.

> "I WAS CONDITIONED TO BELIEVE ANY BOUNDARY I HAD WAS A BETRAYAL OF HER, SO I STAYED SILENT, COOPERATIVE." – JENNETTE MCMURDY, AUTHOR

Enmeshment occurs when there is a lack of independence, excessive involvement between family members, and limited or no boundaries. Each family member melds into the next until there is no clear sense of individuality, but instead, a family unit that looks like one of Frankenstein's creations. It is ugly and dangerous. Note: enmeshment does not always involve all family members and may occur between two or more individuals in the family unit.

Take the lack of individuality and add inappropriate or weak boundaries into the mix, and you have a recipe that creates high tension, mixed messages, and a suffocating environment. Children in enmeshed homes are programmed to ignore their emotions and thoughts while taught to focus on the needs of others.

If mom is happy, you are allowed to exhibit happiness. But if mom is sad, you better join in the pity party. There will be no place for any joy you may be experiencing at that time. Instead, you learn to mimic mom's feelings and lock away all positive emotions. This is done to conform with what you believe is mom's wishes and to protect yourself from her disappointment or wrath.

In an enmeshed home, there is no autonomy, just the development of a group-think mentality. The home atmosphere may be rigid and driven by an overabundance of rules that must be strictly adhered to by each member. But in all cases, emotional manipulation is front and center, and children learn to respond to stabilize a parent's mood.

"I learned at an early age to mirror mom's emotions," said Gerard, who still struggles with porn at age 57. "Because if you did not, there was hell to pay. She would throw tantrums or shut you out. It was painful, so I learned to go with the flow."

But the enmeshed family's most destructive consequence is the loss of self. There is no encouragement for the development of individuality or distinctiveness. Instead, autonomy is eradicated, and individual growth is stifled. Eventually, children relinquish their identities to appease their parents. It is a tragic situation.

There is nothing secure about the attachment found in an enmeshed family.

ENMESHED PARENT TYPES

In her book, *The Emotional Incest Syndrome: What to Do When a Parent's Love Rules Your Life,* Dr. Patricia Love, highlights four parent types in the enmeshed family.

1. The Romanticizing Parent
2. The Neglectful Parent
3. The Abusive and Critical Parent
4. The Sexualizing Parent

The Romanticizing Parent uses a child as a surrogate spouse, sharing inappropriate and intimate information that leaves the child confused and sometimes even guilty that he is betraying the other parent. This behavior is also known as emotional incest.

The Neglectful Parent forces a child to grow up and take on adult responsibilities far too early. Often referred to as childhood lost, these kids may serve as the primary caregiver for younger siblings or, in some cases, an ill parent or perhaps a parent struggling with an illness, addiction, or a mental disorder.

The Abusive and Critical Parent is like Dr. Jekyll and Mr. Hyde. One moment, the parent is kind and sweet, and the next, raging and criticizing. This negative behavior also may be witnessed in the other parent, who may become belligerent and resentful of the child's relationship with the first parent.

The Sexualizing Parent in a large majority of cases, does not sexually abuse the child, however, there is a crossing of blurring lines regarding inappropriate or highly suggestive sexual behaviors. For example, a parent walks around naked or playfully teases in a sexually suggestive manner. Again, this caregiver's behavior is another form of emotional incest.

IT IS A MAJOR ISSUE

Each year, thousands of articles are written about enmeshed relationships and families. The topic is covered in movies, television, and other forms of entertainment. Why? Because watching the interactions of an enmeshed family unfold is like witnessing a train wreck. Although it makes your skin crawl, it is not easy to look away. Of the many books written about the subject, these are some of the most popular:

- When He's Married to Mom
- What to do When a Parent's Love Rules Your Life
- Silently Seduced
- How to Break Your Addiction to a Person
- Co-dependent No More

The subject is well scrutinized because it is a troubling family issue that leaves emotional scars and destroys people's lives.

TEDDY'S STORY

"My mother was a trying person," said Teddy, a single, 56-year-old advertising sales manager with a fondness for high-priced escorts and porn.

When Teddy was 6, his father divorced his mother, and Teddy never saw his father again. An only child, he was attached to his mother's hip as a child and teen. Not that he wanted to be so tightly connected, but he had no choice because his mother would not allow him to experience autonomy.

But the Enmeshed Family's Most Troubling Feature Is the Loss of Self

"Mother never let me out of her sight, except when I went to school, and she headed to work," he recalled. "I was a popular kid in school, but my mom would not let me socialize with other kids or join athletic teams. She said she needed me to be around because she would be lonely."

Starting around age 10, Teddy's mother engaged him in strange conversations, telling him he had to beware of girls because they wanted to take him away from her. She would make him promise that he would never leave her, and rewarded him with sweets and toys each time he made these promises. As time passed, his mother continued using emotional manipulation to keep Teddy from wanting to seek a life outside the home.

"I wanted to play Little League and on the school baseball team, but Mother never allowed it," he said. "Whenever I bought home paperwork, she would raise her voice, telling me I was a selfish son who did not care if his mother was left alone.

"I would feel horrible as her yelling turned to tears, and she asked why I didn't love her," he said with his head lowered. "It was so confusing. She made me feel guilty for wanting to be a kid. So, finally, I gave in and stopped requesting to go places or do things with other kids. I guess I surrendered to her."

But there also was a dark side to Teddy's relationship with his mother that involved sexual incest. "After my dad left, Mother sold my bedroom set and moved me into her room," he said. "And that is where I slept until I graduated college and left home to take a job."

Teddy recalls his mother being sexually flirtatious with him starting at an early age. "She would come out of the shower wearing only a towel and drop it on the floor as she walked into the bedroom," he said. "It wasn't uncommon for her to walk around in her underwear. Or flash her breasts at me."

Teddy's mother also introduced him to porn. "I was 13 when she gave me a copy of Penthouse," he recalled. "After that, she always brought home porn magazines, some very hardcore."

I have elected not to share any additional information regarding his mother's inappropriate and disturbing sexual behaviors toward her son to prevent triggering readers.

According to a Journal of Interpersonal Violence study, most incest offenders report experiencing disappointment and frustration in their marital relationships. Offenders also explained a need for closeness and acceptance drove their actions. Both explanations may have played a role in the actions of Teddy's mother.

EMOTIONAL STRONGHOLD

Over the years, Teddy learned to adjust his mood to whatever his mother felt. "I think she was very depressed because she was often sad. I would hold her as she cried and say she didn't know what to do without me and that I was the only person she could trust.

"By the time I entered high school, I was nothing more than an extension of Mother," he said. "She pressured me to earn my college degree online because she couldn't bear the thought of me leaving her. I remember wanting to go to college, but I did not mention the subject when she started talking about online schools. I knew it would be hopeless to fight her."

In her book, *When You and Your Mother Can't Be Friends: Resolving the Most Complicated Relationship of Your Life,* author Victoria Secunda discusses how anger emerges as children gain more insight into the abuse they endured at the hands of a self-centered parent. *"When we recognize that we are not responsible for our childhood deprivations and that we are entitled to feel anger (but not to act on it - awareness is not a license to kill), then we can let go of that anger and not be controlled by it."*

KEY CHARACTERISTICS OF THE ENMESHED CHILD

Let us examine some of the key characteristics that exist with Enmeshed Children and the issues they face growing up.

- You feel responsible for managing the emotions of others, especially their happiness
- There are no emotional or physical boundaries with others
- You continuously put the needs of others before yours

- You cannot say no to others
- You are confused about your own identity and who you are
- You tend to take on the emotions of others, causing severe mood swings
- You are made to suffer tremendous guilt when you want to lean toward your own needs
- Your caregivers focus on your accomplishments
- You have irrational feelings of guilt
- You have no privacy
- You struggle to make decisions
- No one encourages you to be curious and seek out your interests and desires
- One or both parents treat you like a friend or surrogate spouse, sharing inappropriate information
- You have a fear you will never be able to live up to your parents' expectations

KID TALK

If you resonate with this Inner Child, there are several major focus points involved in your recovery:

1. Discover your identity
2. Remove the negative narratives you believe about yourself
3. Learn to be more assertive and focus on your own needs

Determining your identity (or true self) will take time, but you start by uncovering your needs, wants, and desires. You have spent far too long focusing on what everyone demands from you, but this is a new beginning. Your Inner Child fears disappointing people and not being proactive in recognizing their needs. The Child will continue to push you toward putting yourself second to everyone else.

You must become mindful of the Inner Child's moods and let him know you are in charge and can handle this new way of living. It may be difficult initially, but do not let setbacks derail you. Instead, stay focused on your objective: loving yourself and growing.

Getting rid of negative self-talk will be a challenge as your Child attempts to correct the new attitude you are developing. Having lived through the barrage of hurtful statements made when you failed to put others first, your Inner Child will struggle to believe there is benefit in the positive narratives you are attempting to implement.

But that is all right because, once again, you are in control of this new situation. Your Inner Child should settle down with you, leading the way in establishing the new individual you are becoming. Your positive demeanor may not rub off on the Child, but it certainly will get him to stop and notice that something is different, and with that comes a good deal of comfort for him and you.

Attempting to stand up for yourself may be challenging when you start healing using the Inner Child Model™. The changes you seek to make will feel unnatural. At times, you might find yourself slipping back and seeking to cater to the needs of others at the expense of your desires. That is natural. When you fail to stand up for yourself, do not beat yourself up, but instead determine what led to letting down your guard.

Most likely, your Inner Child became active, and you were unaware of it. Reset and learn from your mistakes so you can do better next time. This is an imperfect journey.

Building a support team, you can trust while seeking assistance when recovery becomes challenging will be your best investment. Instead of trying to determine whether your emotions are accurate or not, you can bounce them off others who can provide you with objective and well-intended advice. You do not, nor should you, go down this critical pathway alone. It is one you travel with others.

Core Emotional Triggers of the Enmeshed Inner Child

This is only a partial list, and you may identify additional triggers. Remember, his emotions occur based on the way he perceives a current situation. However, his perception of evens may be inccurate.

I am confused	I feel lost
I feel unheard	I feel overwhelmed
I do not care	I feel numbed
I feel smothered	I feel guilty

What Core Emotional Triggers did you select?

TAKE A MOMENT: Write about being raised in an enmeshed environment. How do you believe it impacted your relationships as an adult? What do you want to change about yourself moving forward?

CHAPTER 14

Reason 11: The Spiritually Wounded Child

"Time heals everything, that's what everyone says. Wounds heal and leave only scars behind. But some wounds run too deep to heal and pierce the deepest layers of one's soul. They stay there unhealed and ready to ooze blood at the first sign of grief."

—Neena H. Brar, author

Spiritual wounding can be the most crushing form of abuse because it impedes the development of an individual's relationship with his higher power or God. Those who have been spiritually abused have been subjected to behaviors such as:

- Receiving false and manipulating spiritual teachings
- Abusive behaviors, including mental, emotional, sexual, or physical

- Instructed to keep secrets to protect a religious leader or organization
- Restricted from participating in activities under the guise of avoiding worldly temptations
- Shamed to believe God is disappointed and unaccepting of them

"Spiritual wounding is, essentially, the violation of the sacred or spiritual core in human beings, harm experienced at the deepest level of one's being," wrote Edward Kruk, Ph.D., and associate professor at the University of British Columbia's School of Social Work in his paper Spiritual Wounding and Affliction: Facilitating Spiritual Transformation in Social Justice Work.

"When one's life is damaged or destroyed by some wound or privation due to others' actions or negligence, deep wounding may occur that, in a sense, goes far beyond physical harm, social exclusion, and psychological torment but is contained in all of these," continues Kruk. "The state of spiritual affliction transcends all other forms of suffering and induces an inertia such that those experiencing the condition are typically viewed as responsible for their situation, and the social conditions that lead to spiritual harm are largely ignored."

"When I was eight, my parents went to a Bob Gothard seminar called Institute in Basic Life

Principles," said Tate, who was in counseling for having multiple affairs and porn. "They came home, removed the television and radios from the house, and threw away all my toys. I was also told I would be homeschooled and unable to hang out with my friends.

"I was devastated," continued Tate, who has an only child. "I had no idea what was happening all I know is my life had been flipped upside down. We started having family meetings at dinner, where my father talked about the evil outside our house and how we had to protect ourselves by not allowing it to enter our home.

"I was terrified, and I watched as they went from room to room every night praying for God to remove any evil spirits that may have sneaked into our house," he recalled, providing insights into his spiritual abuse. "I grew up isolated and did not go out unless one of my parents was with me. Then, in my junior year, my father announced he was leaving my mother for another woman. Talk about crazy."

Tate would outline how his mother turned completely against Bob Gothard's principles after his father left. The television and radios came back into the house, and Tate was sent off to public school.

"As you can imagine, I was lost among the kids," he said. "I stood out like a sore thumb in the way I dressed, acted, and what I didn't know about pop culture. I had been in a cocoon for years in an attempt to protect myself from the world, and now I was thrown back into it."

Tate endured much teasing from his peers during his last two high school years.

DESECRATED SAFE HAVENS

In their book, The Subtle Power of Spiritual Abuse: Recognizing and Escaping Spiritual Manipulation and False Spiritual Authority Within the Church, Jeff Van Vonderen and David Johnson defined spiritual abuse as:

"The mistreatment of a person who is in need of help, support, or greater spiritual empowerment, with the result of weakening, undermining, or decreasing that person's spiritual empowerment."

As you have read throughout this book, children require safety and need sincere and good-willed people to guide their development. Unfortunately, for many children who later will deal with addictive behaviors, this safety valve was not available. Instead, they were misguided, manipulated, controlled, abused, or coerced by those responsible for providing them with a firm and authentic spiritual foundation.

This scenario provides another example of how some children had to fend for themselves when navigating the emotional distresses and pain people and circumstances tossed at them.

These issues involve conflicts with siblings, bullying at school, appearance concerns, or being ignored or shamed by peers. Because they do not have many worldly experiences and are more emotionally based on their thinking, managing these painful circumstances can take an enormous mental and emotional toll on children.

Having a safe outlet to share their worries and concerns is essential to lower anxiety and reduce the intensity of negative noise in a child's mind. One source some children turn to for help is spiritual leaders – especially youth pastors – who can play a valuable role in their lives, helping them to navigate youthful storms and challenges.

However, instead of finding comfort and wisdom in these leaders, children sometimes experience more harm at the hands of those who are supposed to care for and nurture them.

Abusive Leaders

Some spiritual leaders use their positions of authority to intimidate, condemn, groom, manipulate, or abuse children because of their vulnerability. As they get older, this can result in children isolating themselves from where they should have been taught love is central to all things – the church.

Religious leaders and the church can have a powerful and controlling influence on families and the rules and routines adopted in the home during a child's critical developmental years. Many traditions exist in every religious denomination, including prayers, devotions, saying a blessing at meals, and celebrating religious holy days.

"My parents belonged to a church that was more of a cult," said Zach, a 41-year-old married father of two, who was not exposed to pornography until his mid-20s but soon after

found himself viewing it several times daily. *"It was a small church that had control over how parents raised their children,"* Zach recalled. *"I remember a family who was forced to send their 14-year-old daughter to live with family members in another state because she was caught drinking beer. The church said she was a cancer to other children. That put a lot of fear into me — which is what I think they were trying to do to all the kids — that I better behave, or I would also be sent off."*

Fortunately, few families go to churches as extreme as Zach experienced. Instead, most religious leaders called to their respective ministries are enthusiastic about spreading their faith and helping those in need. Their congregations place great trust in them, and often, these leaders are given significant standing in the community and upheld as honorable and righteous.

> ONE'S DIGNITY MAY BE ASSAULTED AND VANDALIZED, BUT IT CAN NEVER BE TAKEN AWAY UNLESS IT IS SURRENDERED." —MICHAEL J. FOX

The potential for serious issues happens when spiritual leaders are given power with little oversight in dealing with children and teens in their congregations. This is evidenced by the revelation of decades of sexual abuse by religious leaders, especially in the Catholic Church. However, abuse has not been limited to one religious denomination. It occurs in churches worldwide and can take many forms, including physical, verbal, and emotional abuse.

Religious Trauma

Spiritual leaders are not the only ones who rain down abuse on children in the name of spirituality. Parents and other family members can also use religious laws or Scriptures to control a child's actions. And if a child pushes back, these family members will tap into the child's guilt and shame to keep them in line.

Some parents point to biblical Scripture to persuade their children that activities such as attending a school dance or wearing jewelry are prohibited, labeling them lustful. Religious leaders often use the following Scripture to manipulate and restrict the activities of children and teens. *"So, flee youthful passions and pursue righteousness, faith, love, and peace, along with those who call on the Lord from a pure heart"* 2 Timothy 2:22.

The potential damage to a child by parents or religious leaders who are overzealous in their spiritual doctrines, teachings, and rules can be devastating. This type of trauma is so severe it has been recognized by mental health professionals who refer to it as Religious Trauma Syndrome (RTS).

RTS occurs when individuals deal with the psychological aftershocks of exposure to shame-filled and guilt-producing spiritual teachings, authoritarian leaders, and corrupt religious doctrines.

"RTS is a condition experienced by people struggling with leaving an authoritarian, dogmatic religion and coping with the damage of indoctrination," writes Dr. Marlene Winell in her book Leaving the Fold: A Guide for Former Fundamentalists and Others Leaving Their Religion.

Dr. Winell, an expert in RTS, continues, "They may be going through the shattering of a personally meaningful faith and/or breaking away from a controlling community and lifestyle."

Connor is a perfect example of a child who experienced RTS. "My parents did not have a good relationship, and they were very distant," said the 54-year-old electrician who came to therapy sober of PSBs but struggling to connect with his wife emotionally. "Until I was seven, I didn't know what church was, and then it became mom's world in the blink of an eye. Soon, my two sisters and I found ourselves in church six times a week. And that didn't include Bible camps, social activities, or retreats. My entire life revolved around the church.

"The problem with all of it was mom didn't go to church to develop a relationship with God or to educate us about Christianity," he said, his voice growing slightly angry as he recalled this trying time. "She went to escape being at home with our father. She was a hypocrite who didn't abide by religious teachings outside the church.

"She drank too much, cursed, yelled at the three of us constantly, and was a lousy mother," he went on explaining about his life away from the church. "But worse was her belief that God was telling her the rules we needed to follow. God told her what television programs we could watch, what clothes to wear, what friends we could have, and how our hair should look. There were rules for everything.

"As I got older, it made me sick to watch her phoniness on display for the church folks," he concluded, throwing himself back on the couch, exhausted. "I grew to hate her and God."

TYPES OF SPIRITUAL ABUSE

A child can endure numerous types of spiritual abuse at the hands of others, leading to long-term mental and emotional ramifications. These can include:

- Using guilt, shame, and religious rules to control
- Manipulating by claiming to speak on behalf of God
- Holding themselves up as holier than others
- Using Scripture to justify abuse
- Non-compromising religious indoctrination
- Blaming sinful nature on a child's lack of faith
- Providing mental, emotional, and sexual abuse

CHARLIE'S STORY

Charlie grew up in a large Catholic family with a father who was a great provider but offered little guidance and mentorship to his son. In search of a male role model, Charlie eliminated the priests in his church who he saw as unapproachable, mean, and distanced. So, Charlie became one of the many children with nowhere to turn when circumstances become frightening. And in fourth grade, that is precisely what happened.

Charlie attended a Christian academy associated with the church he and his family attended. An older female lay teacher fondled Charlie nearly daily during that school year.

Scared, he felt he had nowhere to turn. His father was unavailable emotionally, and the priests were far too scary. They walked around in black with white collars and emoted a sense of being unapproachable. To Charlie, the last thing they wanted to hear was a young boy claiming to be sexually molested. Besides, he reasoned to himself, they would never believe him.

The abuse left Charlie with many negative narratives, including *"I am bad"* and *"God can't love me."* He became an altar boy to gain some sense of affirmation and be seen as a 'good kid.'

Working behind the church scenes, Charlie had more exposure to the clergy, and what he saw and heard made him more confused. These men held up as leaders, holy and righteous, showed another side to Charlie: being verbally abusive and telling the altar boys they were sinful and going to hell.

> **THESE INNER CHILDREN DEAL WITH SIGNIFICANT SELF-DOUBT AND GUILT, WHICH CAN BE EASILY TRIGGERED IF THEY SENSE SOMEONE IS UNHAPPY WITH THEM**

Feeling he did not meet God's standards because of the sexual abuse he endured and the rhetoric from the priests about his lack of salvation, Charlie battled with depression and thoughts of self-loathing.

At 13, he experienced pornography for the first time while babysitting at a neighbor's home. He soon viewed it multiple times a day and never thought to seek help by bringing it to his father's or the priests' attention because he had been told: *"sinners go to hell."* Charlie felt he could not tell anyone about his desire for porn.

A LIFE OF SHAME

Over the years, he stayed in the endless cycle of viewing porn, experiencing shame, and developing deceptive tools to keep it secret. As the porn intensified, his self-hatred grew, and he started to cut himself. He also started using tobacco and sniffing glue.

And when he married at age 24, nothing changed. Charlie continued watching porn and masturbated several times daily to distract himself from the idea that God hated him and that he was hellhound. After 14 years of marriage, Charlie's wife discovered his secret devotion to porn. It answered many questions for her, especially surrounding their lackluster love life.

"My wife thought I was a good man," Charlie said. "But I disappointed her just as I disappointed God and myself. She finally saw the ugliness I had been trying to hide for years. I was exposed."

KEY CHARACTERISTICS OF THE SPIRITUALLY WOUNDED CHILD

The following explains the development of the Spiritually Wounded Child

- Raised in a legalistic, rigid environment driven by religious rules and regulations
- Taught to have an unhealthy fear of God
- Identity formed through performance
- Struggle to trust others and God
- Suffer various abuses at the hands of church leaders
- Deal with self-loathing and perhaps engage in self-harm
- Lack of confidence in their ability to make decisions

INNER CHILD THEORY IN ACTION

In therapy, Charlie understood his porn addiction was a coping strategy to help him quiet down the negative noise that he was a bad person. He discovered that current events that remind him of his unresolved childhood pain points triggered his Inner Child.

Charlie was shown how to allow himself to experience the emotional discomfort he suffered in the past, including the sexual abuse, without turning to distractions. He discovered he could handle negative distress and did not need to turn to porn for comfort.

He worked hard to identify the core emotional triggers that would activate his Inner Child and lead him to use porn and masturbation for soothing. The negative internal messages Charlie struggled with were:

- I am bad when I think about sex
- I cannot do anything right

- I am dirty
- I am unlovable
- God hates me
- I am worthless

During treatment, he also realized he had no idea what emotional intimacy or healthy sexuality looked like. His childhood experiences with the church, including being sexually abused, left him feeling uncomfortable and ashamed of the topic. In addition, the young Charlie also learned about sex and love by watching porn.

Charlie started to attend Emotions Anonymous to learn how to identify and express his emotions. Through bibliotherapy (therapy through reading), he discovered the keys to developing authentic sexual intimacy. We also arranged weekly meetings with a local pastor who taught Charlie the positive benefits of living a Christian life and the power of God's Grace.

Three years after starting therapy, Charlie reports he is still abstemious from porn and masturbation and feels much better about himself and his relationship with God. He also attends Emotions Anonymous and reports that his marriage continues to improve.

KID TALK

If you resonate with this Inner Child, patience will be a critical virtue to develop. These Inner Children deal with significant self-doubt and guilt, which can be easily triggered if they sense someone is unhappy with them. Their ears will be ringing with the negative comments and criticism they received from those in authority growing up.

The Child must also sift through and understand the truths and lies regarding religion. You may need to uncover more information about God and His nature. It can help you and your Child to realize God is not only all-powerful, but He is love. He is full of Grace that He offers His children, and He accepts and loves them unconditionally. But what is so comforting is knowing you are one of His children. Do you know what your Inner Child wants most? Comfort. It is a win-win.

As with all these Inner Children, learning to sit with the negative emotions this Child throws your way is vital. You must slow down the Child by spending time sorting through his negative emotions (what you feel) and processing them through the reality of your life today (what is real). Remember, your Inner Child is trapped in a time warp – your past – surrounded by negative circumstances, people, and emotions.

The Child intermingles hurtful emotional events from the past with events you experience today. But in most cases, he gets it wrong. In most cases, what happened in the past does not match the event/s occurring today. It just FEELS that way. And what you feel vs. what is real are usually vastly different things. That last statement is the most profound and helpful you will find in this entire book. I hope you are discovering many helpful things as you read but implementing "what you feel vs. what is real" daily will help change your life dramatically.

It would be extremely helpful to point out to the Inner Child your accomplishments — no matter how small they may seem — to reassure the Child that you are in control. You want your Inner Child to understand that an authority figure (you) will provide him with a safe environment. And that decisions will no longer be made based on raw emotions but on a more stable platform of rational thinking. Remember, what you feel vs. what is real is usually entirely different things.

Core Emotional Triggers
of the Spiritually Wounded Child

This is only a partial list, and you may identify additional triggers. Remember, his emotions occur based on the way he perceives a current situation. However, his perception of evens may be incurate.

I am dirty	I feel unaccepted
I feel damaged	I feel manipulated
I feel conflicted	I feel controlled
I feel unloved	I feel lost

What Core Emotional Triggers did you select?

TAKE A MOMENT: Write about your spiritual wounds as a child. How do you believe it impacted your life as an adult? What do you want to change about yourself moving forward?

CHAPTER 15
Reason 12: The Unwanted Child

Belonging. Child developmental specialists understand having a sense of belonging is one of the strongest needs a kid must experience to generate and maintain healthy and vibrant relationships. Without this basic foundational pillar, children will struggle to develop a strong sense of self and constantly question their value.

As adults, their inability to belong and fit in has led to many relational issues. Knowing you belong is a survival need that

is met when others establish a connection and communicate you are wanted and accepted. This need is so powerful because we were designed to be in relationship with others.

"For if they fall, one will lift up his fellow. But woe to him who is alone when he falls and has not another to lift him up!" Ecclesiastes 4:10

"Since the earliest period of our life was preverbal, everything depended on emotional interaction," writes John Bradshaw in his best-selling book Healing the Shame that

Binds You. "Without someone to reflect our emotions, we had no way of knowing who we were."

And therefore, as an adult, this Child will always struggle to feel loved even by those who love them. Their lack of trust requires them to erect an invisible barrier that allows loved ones to get only so close. Their fear is if anyone were to connect fully, that individual would be mortified by the ugliness the Unwanted Child carries. Their unfortunate worldview is *"no one could truly love me because I am unlovable."* Potential romantic partners and friends may recognize the Unwanted Child wounds exhibited, and may be reluctant to invest in starting relationships, sensing barriers and obstacles to establishing meaningful and healthy connections.

UNWANTED. REALLY?

It is difficult to imagine parents who would not want to have endearing and heartfelt relationships with their children. Most adults possess a drive and desire to love, protect, nurture, and develop innocent and adventurous children. It seems natural we would aspire to be part of a child's journey to become a well-adjusted person.

Is it possible some kids are truly unwanted by their parents, or are these cases of children who are oversensitive or extremely needy? Unfortunately, the answer is far too many children are born to people who do not desire or deserve the title of parents.

"I can remember being 10 or 11 and wandering the neighborhood going from house to house to talk with any mother who would listen to me," said Felix, a 52-year-old married construction worker who has been using dating apps for 20 years to engage in emotional and sexual affairs with women. "I didn't know my father, and my mother never kept track of me. I went home to sleep but spent most of my time at other people's homes.

"And what a flirt I was," he said excitedly as he continued to explain his youthful pursuit of mature women. "It was ridiculous. I was trying to get these women to kiss and hug me, and occasionally I would touch their breasts. How insane was it for a young child to aggressively seek affection from older women? And since I have been married, I keep chasing women to feel as though I am wanted."

Felix deals with a tremendous abandonment issue due to the lack of bonding with an absent father and neglectful mother. Hungry for connection, he sought out neighborhood women who saw him as a cute but "naughty" young boy because of his aggressive pursuit to be physical with them.

In the meantime, his mother, who alienated herself from other women in the closely-knit Brooklyn, NY neighborhood, carried on her life as though her son barely existed. She provided him with shelter, clothing, and some money, but that was the extent of her involvement with her son.

AS AN ADULT, THIS CHILD WILL ALWAYS STRUGGLE TO FEEL LOVED EVEN BY THOSE WHO DO LOVE THEM

"When I was 14, I got involved in a sexual relationship with one of the neighborhood women," continued Felix, who has been cheating on his wife throughout their 27-year marriage. "She was probably in her 30s and divorced. I could not get enough of her because she made me feel special. I had never felt special before."

Like many other boys raised by an unavailable mother, Felix wondered what was wrong with him that he could not receive the love and nurturing a child requires from his parents. This emotional torment and confusion lead children to develop various coping strategies, such as the one Felix utilized (aggressively seeking out nurturing) to overcome feelings of inadequacy.

A parent can't hide their true emotions from the Unwanted Child. Beyond their destructive words and actions, a parent's tonality, body language, and facial expressions continually provide the child with the indirect message, *"I wish you were not here."* Dealing with this dreaded reality, a child eventually identifies with the parents' rejection and assumes there are valid reasons for the parents' hatred. In turn, the child starts to see himself – and not the parents – as the problem and begins the internal process of tormenting himself. He sides with the parent and engages in self-hatred and perhaps self-abuse. He believes nothing good can be found in him, and his new identity has been packaged and sealed. He has set the stage for a life of continuous pain and disappointment.

There are numerous reasons a child may feel unwanted, ranging from neglect to being adopted. We will examine some of the rationales during the course of this chapter as we take an in-depth look at these unfortunate children and the mental and emotional pain they are destined to experience.

THE DISTANCE MOTHER

Mothers serve as ground zero for children's early emotional and mental development. A mother plays a substantial role in determining if a child will possess a healthy attachment style and be able to successfully bond with others throughout life. Yes, motherhood comes with great responsibility, and much depends upon their attitude in serving as a nurturing source for their sons.

Unfortunately, many women do not possess natural mothering instincts and are complete failures when securing healthy attachments with their children. Some mothers are anything but maternal, whether it be their lack of nurturing skills, mental or physical limitations, addictions, or past traumas and neglect. And it is their dysfunctional ways that can lead to generations of families suffering from relational strains.

Some of the reasons a mother may distance herself from a child include the following:

- Unwanted pregnancies such as accidental, rape, affair-produced, early age pregnancy, etc.
- Anchor baby who was conceived to keep a marriage together
- An ill infant or child who has health issues or disabilities that overwhelm the parent

- Limited capacity to love, which results in the mother having a favorite child who receives all of her affection, leaving nothing for others

When a mother withdraws, is emotionally distanced, or completely ignores her son, she sets the stage for the development of a man who will find it difficult to attach in healthy ways with other women. Instead of being a secure, confident man who can provide a woman with a safe and loving relationship, he may instead become:

- Co-dependent in relationships, sacrificing his own emotional needs in an attempt to keep his partner happy and content
- Emotionally undeveloped and lacking the skills necessary to create a satisfying relationship with his partner
- Inwardly focused, demanding his needs become a top priority for his partner
- Angry toward women, possibly become an abuser lashing out emotionally, mentally, physically, and sexually
- Untrusting and closed off to others, putting up an invisible wall to keep people at a distance
- Engaged in relationships with toxic and abusive people

THE UNAVAILABLE FATHER

Fathers who have abandoned their families have been a topic of importance since the 1960s. According to the National

Fatherhood Initiative, an organization that provides research on father presence and involvement, it is estimated in the U.S., more than 18 million children – or 1 in 4 – live without a biological, step, or adoptive father in the home. And according to 2019 Census Bureau data, 7 million men are completely absent from their children's lives.

"I never met my father," said Sam, who is single, 27 years old, and has dealt with a porn issue since he was 12. "My mother told me my dad decided not to marry her when she got pregnant and left the state. I am unsure if I ever missed him, but I want to know him today. But I would not even know where to start to look."

Homes without a father figure dramatically increase the risk of a child dealing with negative social, educational, or legal issues. That is not to say single mothers cannot raise well-adjusted men; instead, it indicates it could be more challenging depending on numerous factors, including the socio-economic conditions of families.

Again, this is not to say all boys raised without fathers are subjected to a difficult childhood with little chance of becoming well-adjusted adults. However, being raised in a home without a father limits a boy's opportunity to see the model of what it means to be a man. And that can lead to serious challenges as an adult.

"Every woman I have dated has told me I am immature and have no clue how to be a man," said Stanley, who is 44 and has never been married and struggles with porn. "All my relationships are short-lived, maybe 4 to 6 months tops. Growing up, I did not have a father and was raised by my mom as the only boy among four kids. They did everything for me, and I still expect that from women today. But it doesn't happen. I don't know if I will ever get it right."

UNWANTED CHILDREN CREATE UNHEALTHY COPING MECHANISMS TO MASK THEIR EMOTIONAL PAIN

Not all absentee fathers abandon their families. Some remain present but do not emotionally engage. This may mean the father emotionally neglects all of the children or just one child.

"My father rejected me," said Lonny, who, at 47, recently went through his second divorce. Both resulted from his infidelity and excessive spending on prostitutes and strip clubs, which led to family financial woes. *"I mean unless he was criticizing me. That seemed to be the only time I received his attention.*

"What was really hurtful was to see him interact with my sister and brother in a caring way," said Lonny, whose personality assessment showed an avoidant attachment wound that prevented him from fully bonding with others. *"Around age nine, I decided I would not allow him to hurt me, so I shut down emotionally. I was tired of waiting for the day he would take me in his arms and tell me how much he loved me. Instead, I decided that day will never come, and I don't want it anyway."*

Unwanted Children like Lonny ultimately create unhealthy coping mechanisms to mask their emotional pain. Since his father caused him emotional distress, Lonny subconsciously decided he would return the favor by getting in trouble at school and with the law.

"Something happened that day. I decided to stop hoping for my father's love, which turned my world upside down," Lonny recalled. "I became a bad student, failing all of my classes. At 16, I dropped out of school. But I also got into a lot of legal trouble, including causing property damage on a regular basis. It cost my father a small fortune to pay for the damage I did and attorney fees. When I think about it, I guess it was my payback for the hell he put me through."

Lonny last saw his father when he was 17 and left home to join the Army. He never went back and lost contact with all of his family members. That was a heavy price to pay for a young man with much hatred in his heart. And Lonny is still paying the price today with his reckless actions.

GUARDIANS

Sometimes, the Unwanted Child is raised by someone other than his parents. Instead, the boy is entrusted to another relative or perhaps a nanny.

"My mother was a trust-fund brat who had me via artificial insemination," said Mark, who at 35 had just experienced his third divorce. All of them ended as a result of his numerous affairs. "I do not have many memories of my mother growing up. Adair was my nanny, and she cared for me 24/7 while my mother was jet-setting across the globe, partying with her elite friends. I saw her maybe three or four days a month, and even then, she did not spend much time with me."

Although usually placed in the hands of responsible and caring adults, these children struggle to understand why their parents keep their distance and do not engage in their lives.

"Adair treated me well, but she was not my mother," Mark continued explaining that he was granted much freedom, which allowed him to discover porn at 13. "Why does a woman have a child she does not care about? I'll tell you why. She wanted to brag to her friends that she was a single mother who could maintain her independence.

"And she certainly did that; she was very independent," Mark continued, shaking his head back and forward and becoming more irritable as he spoke. "But she was not a mother. Even today, I see her maybe once a year but never a phone call. There were many gifts sent, but I stopped opening them about nine years ago. They are piled up in a storage unit. They can rot along with her, as far as I am concerned."

These children feel they had been pawned off to someone else by their parents, who did not have an interest in raising them. When parents hand the responsibility of rearing their children to someone else, it is a decision that comes at a terrible price.

"I am not even 40 and divorced three times. I think I will go for Larry King's record," Mark joked about the talk show host who was married eight times and trying to make light of his own less-than-impressive record of accomplishment when it comes to relationships. *"I don't belong in a long-term relationship. They make me anxious, but so does being alone. I hate being alone."*

Like many Unwanted Children, Mark deals with an attachment disorder – anxious-avoidant. Mark desires to connect with someone but has a subconscious fear of abandonment. Therefore, when he marries, he has no intention of being unfaithful. However, as time goes on, he finds himself seeking the attention of other women to quiet his abandonment fears. Mark enters all relationships with one foot in and one foot out. Unfortunately for him and the women who marry him, he is unaware of this tragic dilemma.

THE ADOPTED CHILD

Adoption provides an amazing opportunity for children to be placed in homes with couples who want to share their love and resources. According to the Adoption Network, around 100,000 children are adopted annually in the United States. However, some who are adopted feel they are Unwanted Children, even if the individuals who welcomed them into their homes are warm, caring, and loving. Why is this the case?

Even if adopted as an infant, as children get older and discover they have been adopted, they may experience the emotional anguish of feeling rejected by their natural parents. Although they were "chosen" by their adoptive families, for some, that means first they had to be abandoned. And with this "fact" comes the belief they are Unwanted Children.

"I was very blessed to be raised in the adoptive home I grew up in," said Clay, who was adopted at the age of 2 after his grandmother, who was raising him, died and his mother, a drug addict, could not care for him. *"But that didn't stop me*

from being angry that my mother couldn't get her life together to raise me. Obviously, I wasn't that important to her because if I were, she would not have abandoned me."

With this mindset can come self-condemning thoughts such as *"I wasn't good enough for them"* or *"I didn't meet their expectations."* These are irrational thoughts based on limited or no information about the circumstances of their natural birth parents and their reasons for opting for adoption. But the thinking feels very real.

Identity issues may also confront those who have been adopted. It is common for them to wonder who they were before the adoption or who they should have been. This is especially true if they know nothing about their birth families. Much of this makes sense. These individuals often do not know their ancestors or original family backgrounds. They feel left in the dark, leaving them feeling unwanted.

ISSUES AS ADULTS

The rejection an Unwanted Child experiences in his younger years leaves him with toxic self-worth and a broken compass when it comes to selecting a healthy partner as an adult. Here are some key issues that impact adults who were Unwanted Children.

- **Anxiety and Depression.** It is quite common for Unwanted Children to deal with anxiety and depressed moods. Overwhelmed with a chronic feeling of rejection can drive the adult who resonates with Unwanted Child toward isolation as a coping strategy to deal with emotions centering on negative narratives such as *"I am not good enough"* or *"I am unlovable."* Unfortunately, this practice can lead to a self-fulfilling prophesy that *"I will always be alone."* The anxiety experienced by these men heightens their compulsiveness, which will lead them to continue using the coping strategy they adopted as children to escape from emotional distress — behaviors that can become addictive.

- **Attracting Drama.** Lacking relationships as a young man may lead to being drawn into dysfunctional relationships as an adult. It is common for these men to be addicted to drama when it comes to relationships. Their dysfunction could attract them to toxic, unhealthy people who will make life more difficult. Some individuals they become involved with may be emotionally or mentally abusive.

- **Clinging On.** This behavior finds these men unable to walk away from unhealthy relationships due to their abandonment issues. For some, the concept of bad attention is better than no attention far outweighs the possibility of being alone. Even if they cannot trust the person they are involved with, they may stay in the relationship hoping to change their partner. This desperate attempt for connection often leaves these men enduring numerous heartaches that solidify their low self-worth and keep them feeling unwanted. They find themselves recreating their childhood wounds by allowing themselves to engage with individuals who continue to abuse them emotionally and mentally.

- **Go It Alone**. The Unwanted Child tends to be in relationships with little or no emotional connection as an adult. There may be warm bodies around, but they are making little or no effort to engage. This is because the Unwanted Child usually lacks the skills to nurture a relationship.

- **Compromising Values.** Some Unwanted Children who feel they do not fit in may take extremely aggressive and reckless actions to be accepted. "Whatever It Takes" could be their mantra and may lead to compromising their self, beliefs, and values. There is enormous pressure in today's society to belong; if that is not accomplished, it may erode an individual's self-worth.

- **Narcissism 101.** A young boy feeling unwanted and unloved may try to mask these feelings by creating a false persona rooted in self-absorption and raging pride. This can lead to an individual who manipulates, deceives, and uses others for personal gain. They are cunning and often come across as compassionate and caring individuals, but they believe it is their turn to come out on top.

KID TALK

Making efforts to validate your Inner Child's pain of feeling unwanted and unloved is something you should focus on during those times when a Core Emotional Trigger is NOT activating the Child. Trying to nurture the Child when he is active will not go well. During those times, he is not receptive to nurturing and is focused solely on running off to get comfort from what he knows works — PSBs or other destructive behaviors.

When your Inner Child is quiet, you can spend time working to ensure he is wanted and loved. Most importantly, he must understand that you — as an adult — are there to protect him from the emotions of feeling unwanted. Also, please ensure the Child understands there never was anything wrong with him, but instead, the fault lies with those adults who did not provide him with the nurturing he required.

Core Emotional Triggers of the Unwanted Child

This is only a partial list, and you may identify additional triggers. Remember, his emotions occur based on the way he perceives a current situation. However, his perception of evens may be inccurate.

I feel confused	I feel alone
I feel abandoned	I feel empty
I feel discarded	I feel unlovable
I feel anxious	I feel depressed

What Core Emotional Triggers did you select?

TAKE A MOMENT: If you resonate with this Inner Child, write about your experiences of feeling unwanted. What led to those emotions you experienced? Do you sometimes still feel that way today?

CHAPTER 16

Now You Know. So, What's Next?

So, what do you think so far? Have you uncovered any insights on which core emotional triggers may activate your Inner Child? Have you been pondering the **why** question about your PSBs and their origin? Have you tried to communicate with your Inner Child?

Hopefully, what you have read thus far has made considerable inroads in those directions for you. But if not, it is ok. This is a marathon, not a sprint. In fact, it is sometimes exceedingly difficult to give up our addictive behaviors.

"Addictive compulsive behaviors are attempts to feel better, so it's scary to give them up," writes Andrew Susskind, LCSW, SEP, CGP, in his book It's Not About the Sex, where he provides insights on maintaining sexual sobriety. "It makes you vulnerable. Addictions are also used to regulate your nervous system, so it's crucial to build and strengthen new, effective ways to cope as you give up destructive behaviors."

> **THIS IS A SIMPLE PROCESS; HOWEVER, IT IS NOT EASY TO IMPLEMENT UNLESS YOU COMMIT TO BEING MINDFUL OF WHAT YOUR MIND, EMOTIONS, AND BODY ARE TELLING YOU**

Susskind touches upon a critical point that anyone struggling with addiction must fully comprehend. Addictions serve a purpose. And that purpose is to manage anxiety. Thus far, you have learned that much of your anxiety results from unresolved pain points caused by trauma and neglect. You may be saying, *"I am not an anxious person."* I understand, and for decades, I felt the same way. However, I was wrong. And unfortunately, you are too.

Maintaining a Low Anxiety Level

Leads to Reduced Compulsive Behaviors

Leads to Reduced Poor Behavioral Choices

Children can do an amazing job of repressing their anxiety to the point where they cannot recognize when it is being generated. However, it manifests in other ways, such as anger, passive-aggressiveness, or avoiding conflict. If you reduce your anxiety, in turn, you reduce compulsive behaviors. And ultimately, that leads to a reduction in poor behavioral choices.

A major change you need to make in your life is being aware of your anxiety level daily and, in some cases, hourly. Being cognizant that you are anxious will allow you to take action to lower your tension immediately. *This is critical, so please do not take this advice lightly.* As we move forward in this chapter, we will review techniques to help you manage your anxiety healthily and, therefore, better manage your compulsiveness.

THE ACTIVATED INNER CHILD

With that in mind, let us examine a highly effective method for engaging and soothing your Inner Child and, in turn, managing your PSBs.

Remember, you are attempting to empower yourself by keeping one step ahead of the little boy and his tantrums. Reading on, you certainly will recognize some of the steps in the process covered earlier in this book. You must study these steps thoroughly to be prepared when your Child is activated.

Let us start by reexamining how to determine if your Inner Child has been activated. This process occurs when your anxiety (discomfort) level increases and drives you to escape through stimulating or numbing activities.

Signs the Inner Child is Activated

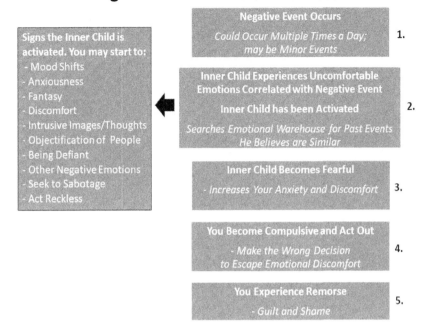

As we explained in Chapter 2, your Inner Child is activated by negative events (step 1), which may happen several times a day. For example:

- You are late for an appointment
- Your favorite pants no longer fit
- You got two hours of sleep
- The boss is not happy
- An unexpected bill is due
- Your wife calls you an idiot
- One of your children is sick
- Checking out at the store, you realize you forgot your wallet
- You are behind in cutting the lawn

- Your dog dies
- You are bored
- Your daughter is in trouble at school
- A driver cuts you off in traffic
- Your favorite sports team lost
- You spill coffee on your shirt
- Your tooth hurts
- The car will not start

The negative event (step 2) reminds your Inner Child of a past event(s) that occurred years ago. Subconsciously, the Child correlates the past event(s) with the current one (although they may not be similar). When this happens, your anxiety level continues to increase (with you believing it is the current event solely responsible for your increased anxiety). Ultimately, discomfort escalates as your Inner Child becomes more fearful, and your compulsiveness (steps 3 & 4) also increases. And off you go, seeking an escape from the emotional pain you learned years ago to avoid, like COVID.

After you are finished running away and return to reality, a sense of remorse (step 5) may appear. However, this does not happen with everyone after sexually acting out. Your Inner Child has once again successfully taken over and dictated your actions.

DEALING WITH YOUR INNER CHILD

So, what do we do with this Inner Child whose fears and inability to sit with emotional discomfort lead us to engage in unwanted behaviors? Answer: we learn to stay one step ahead of him. So, what does this look like? It is all about mindfulness and self-reflection.

The number one skill you will need to develop is being mindful. You will be required to recognize the warning signs your mind, emotions, and body are delivering when the Inner Child is starting to become activated. No longer will you allow yourself to engage in wandering fantasy, mindlessly scrolling on social media, or allowing your eyes and mind to engage in street lust (objectifying others in public). The days of ignoring important physical symptoms such as restlessness and tension are over.

To stay one step ahead of your Inner Child, you must be more alert and aware of your surroundings and mental, emotional, and physical states. And that means rule number one: **Slow Everything Down**. And I mean everything. You cannot afford to continue running through life with your head down and hoping for the best. Instead, you must lift your head high and be diligent about what activates your Inner Child:

1. Core Emotional Triggers
2. Being Drained Mentally, Emotionally, Physically, or Spiritually

5 NECESSARY STEPS

It is time to examine the core of the Inner Child Model and how you can successfully implement it to manage your PSBs. Let us start by examining this chart that highlights the steps.

How to Deal with the Kid

1.	**Know Your Core Emotional Triggers** *Memorize Them*
2.	**Recognize Negative Events** *That Activate Your Inner Child*
3.	**Process the Inner Child's** **Emotional Discomfort**
4.	**Taking Control: Employ Rational Thinking** *What You Feel vs. What is Real*
5.	**Make the Right Choice** *Select Healthy Lifelines*

Inner Child Model™ –Abundant Life Counseling, Highlands, NC

STEP I: KNOW YOUR CORE EMOTIONAL TRIGGERS

As discussed throughout this book, core emotional triggers are responsible for arousing your PSBs. These triggers appear when current negative events occur that your Inner Child correlates with past emotional wounds. These frightening memories lead the Child to become activated and to seek immediate comfort (by searching for a distraction).

Uncovering your core emotional triggers makes you more prone to compulsive behaviors. While you may not immediately be aware of your uncomfortable state, your level of discomfort will increase as the Child becomes more afraid. This fear, in turn, will drive your Inner Child to push you to participate in activities that distract, stimulate, or soothe. And you are not even aware that he exists. You believe your high distress results from the current negative event you experienced.

Think about it. How often have you thought, "Why is this (fill-in-the-blank event) bothering me so much? It's not really a bad deal. But for some reason, it is annoying the hell out of me!" Sound familiar?

It is bothering you because your Inner Child is exasperating the current situation by subconsciously focusing on similar painful circumstances you experienced in the past. He is throwing gas on the fire, and you are about to ignite.

Therefore, the first step in managing your Inner Child is identifying the core emotional triggers that activate him. Clients often ask, *"how do I identify core emotional triggers."* This process occurs when you identify painful and disappointing traumas/neglects endured in childhood and teen years. In learning to sit with the pain you have long ignored, you will pinpoint triggers that activate your Inner Child.

While this work is not easy, it is necessary to trace back and correlate events that generated the core emotional triggers that lead us to seek PSBs as escapes. The key is to understand your past persistently and how it still negatively impacts you today.

As you search for your core emotional triggers, understand there may be many. Although it does happen, having only one emotional trigger rarely exists. It is also important to know in many cases, you will discover you have multiple emotional triggers similar in nature.

For example, if "need for attention" is a core emotional trigger, you may find your Inner Child also activated by other similar emotions, such as feeling abandoned, dismissed, empty, and invisible, to name a few. Those emotions all have a similar "feel," but when experienced, they may seem vastly different.

For example, "I am unnoticed" and "I feel invisible" seem similar, however, to different people, one may be more overpowering. You must sort through similar triggers to determine which one(s) strikes the most sensitive nerve. And those are the ones you become most aware of when they occur.

Once you have identified the core emotional triggers, it is essential to become familiar with them. I recommend writing them on an index card and carrying them with you. Reflect upon them several times a day until you know them by heart. But equally important, you need to understand what you experience when each core emotional trigger appears. Is there a tightening in your chest, an ache in the back of your neck, tingling in your hands and fingers, etc.? In what ways are you anxious? Do you feel restless? Impatient? Angry? Unsafe?

Take time to determine how the core emotional triggers impact your thoughts, emotions, and body so you can more quickly identify that your Inner Child has been activated. Also, refer to the ***Going Deeper Workbook*** for step-by-step instructions on identifying and narrowing down your primary core emotional triggers.

Last point. The rest will fail if you do not get this part of the process right. Understanding your core emotional triggers is vital to comforting the Inner Child and managing your PSBs.

STEP 2: RECOGNIZE NEGATIVE EVENTS

Negative events happen to you throughout the day. Most are minor, and you do not give them another thought after a few seconds. Others, however, are more impactful and can take the bottom out of your day, causing you to crash.

This is especially important – not all negative events activate your Inner Child. How will we know the difference? Because negative events that activate your Inner Child will involve one or more of your core emotional triggers.

That is why you must be alert and evaluate all negative events against the core emotional triggers you have identified to see if there is a correlation. Following me thus far?

A negative event does not need to be tragic. It could be as simple as an old-time friend who cancels a lunch date at the last minute. While you may immediately brush it off as no big deal if one of your core emotional triggers is rejection, your Inner Child may correlate the canceled lunch date with a time as a child when you were alienated or rejected by friends. For example, the time you went to a friend's house and found three of your other friends there already but were told he could not have anyone else in the house as he slammed the door in your face.

THE INNER CHILD REMEMBERS EVERYTHING

Can you recall the disappointment and embarrassment you felt at that moment? If not, rest assured your Inner Child does. And he may be experiencing the same pain due to the canceled lunch, although the circumstances are entirely different. But then again, he is just a kid.

There is nothing rational about how your little guy thinks and processes information. Remember, his thinking is more emotionally based.

So how does your Inner Child's sensing rejection impact you at that moment? It depends. Immediately, there will likely be a slight mood shift — and not for the better. However, as the Child gets caught up in the past event, your discomfort level will increase (thinking it is about the canceled lunch date). As the anxiousness grows, you may find yourself engaging in sexual fantasy, objectifying people around you, or developing feelings of defiance, sadness, or entitlement.

PHYSICAL RAMIFICATIONS

An activated Inner Child will also impact you physically. Remember, his core emotional triggers cause distress and anxiety. When he starts experiencing troubling emotions, they will create uncomfortable physical sensations for you. Being mindful of what your body is feeling can assist you in being aware the Inner Child has become active.

"Trauma victims cannot recover until they become familiar with and befriend the sensations in their body," writes Dr. Bessel Van Der Kolk in his NY Times bestseller entitled, The Body Keeps the Score. "Being frightened means you live in a body that is always on guard. The bodies of child abuse victims are tense and defensive until they find a way to relax and feel safe. To change, people need to become aware of their sensations and how their bodies interact with the world around them. Physical self-awareness is the first step in releasing the tyranny of the past."

LEARNING TO BE MINDFUL IS GOING TO BECOME A HABIT YOU WILL NEED TO DEVELOP MOVING FORWARD

Dr. Van Der Kolk paints a clear picture of the Inner Child in his description of trauma. The Child is frightened and will remain tense until he finds a way to feel safe – escaping utilizing sex. Your Inner Child's tension will result in you experiencing annoying and perhaps painful physical ailments. Dr. Van Der Kolk believes awareness of these troublesome symptoms is essential to overall recovery.

"Simply noticing our annoyance, nervousness, or anxiety immediately helps us shift our perspective and opens us to new options other than our automatic, habitual reactions," he writes. "When we pay focused attention to our bodily sensations, we can recognize the ebb and flow of our emotions and, with that, increase our control over them."

As discussed, you will remain unaware of adverse events that impact your Inner Child if you have not identified your core emotional triggers. In this case, when a negative event activates one of your triggers, you may revert to your childhood solution of seeking to escape by utilizing behaviors that stimulate or numb.

"Avoid the chaos! Runaway!" screams your Inner Child as he tries to protect himself from the perceived emotional distress. And that is precisely what is going on regarding your PSBs. It is nothing more than a coping strategy to protect you from dealing with core emotional triggers. That is why you must start with Step 1 and not only identify your triggers but also imprint them in your mind. This process is about preparation. And the more you prepare for the next triggering event, the more successful you will be in conquering it.

Again, we are not painting the Child as evil. He is trapped in a period where he did not see rational and healthy options during times of trouble – and that mindset still is a challenge for him today. That is why it is up to us to slow everything down, assist him in processing his emotional pain, and then take over the decision-making process by rationally thinking through our circumstances.

So, there is a big problem. How do you control PSBs when you do not know they have been activated? The answer? Again, learn to be mindful.

Step 3: Process the Inner Child's Emotional Discomfort

At this point, we accurately understand what has activated our Inner Child and has him engaging in an emotional tantrum. By reflecting on the current negative event(s) we are experiencing, we will be able to see how the Child correlates it to a painful memory of the past.

Remember earlier the quote from Jay Stringer's book Unwanted, "One way of thinking about unwanted sexual behavior is to see it as the convergence of two rivers: your past and the difficulties you face in the present." That is what Step 3 is about, discovering what event(s) from the past is muddling together with a current negative event that activates your Inner Child.

For example, you forgot to pay the electric bill on time and incurred a late fee. This event probably is not a major negative event on a scale of one to 10, but do not tell your Inner Child. He sees what has happened as incompetency on your part. *"Lazy! Lazy! Lazy! That is what we are – lazy! Lazy people make foolish mistakes!"* That is what the Child is experiencing when the late charge occurs.

Why?

Because he remembers your dad always criticizing you about being lazy and constantly saying you would amount to nothing, and although you have made a good living as a police officer, internally, you feel you have not measured up in your father's eyes. He still tells you it was a mistake not to become an attorney.

At the Root of 'why' Men Suffer from PSBs Is Their Desire Not to Sit with Emotional Discomfort

It is the heartbreak of being a disappointment to daddy that your Inner Child cannot escape. And sometimes, it only takes a minor event – such as not paying your electric bill on time – to make the child experience the feeling of being an inadequate son.

We need to learn to embrace our Inner Child and understand the depth of the pain he endured, whether through direct or indirect messages he received from parents, siblings, peers, and other authority figures that frightened and scarred him. And it is via this new relationship with the Child that we will better understand **why** we think, feel, and act the way we do.

Besides identifying your core emotional triggers, this is the most critical part of the entire process of managing your Inner Child and your PSBs. If you miss this part, the entire process, again, falls apart.

Our inability to sit and experience emotional pain and discomfort got us into this mess. I have yet to meet someone who struggles with addiction (I am talking about all addictions) who can sit and process emotional pain.

You hate emotional distress and will do **ANYTHING** to avoid it. In fact, you cut off many of your deepest emotions at an early age to avoid uncomfortable feelings. But look where that got us. Along with those around us, we have endured tremendous pain and heartache.

If you think about it, it is ironic. As children and teens, we mastered avoiding painful feelings to cope, and now, we discover running away from emotional pain has done nothing but increase our pain points. If we had learned to deal with our emotional distress in healthy ways, we most likely would have avoided developing addictive behaviors. But here we are. So, there is no time like now to learn how to deal with those messy, uncomfortable emotions.

GOING BACK TO THE PAST

In this step of the process, you will sit with your Inner Child and tap into the pain he endures. Let us return to the Inner Child, who believes he disappointed his dad. You must reflect and recall what it felt like to hear dad's harsh and hurtful words. And as you recall the pain from the past, perhaps you also ponder dad's current-day antics of dishing out passive-aggressive comments about not becoming a lawyer. It all hurts. But that is okay. Painful emotions serve a purpose.

"Vulnerability is an essential part of being human, and vulnerabilities are the doorways back into peace, joy, and love," says Mary O'Malley, author of the book What's in the Way Is the Way: A Practical Guide for Waking Up to Life. "The more open your heart is, the more you have access to your natural state of peace, well-being, and ease, no matter what is happening."

Touching the raw nerves connected to past trauma and pain is healthy, although it feels anything but pleasant when you are knee-deep in it. However, one of the most significant benefits you can derive from learning to feel the pain is learning to let go of your PSBs.

Think about it. You are already hurting because of the damage your PSBs have caused to yourself and others. So, if you must suffer, why not focus on the pain that will ultimately benefit your life?

You would be smart to face the difficult and trying emotions that confront you at some point. If not, you will continue to succumb to your Inner Child's desire to seek comfort and escape through destructive behaviors. And when he wins, your loved ones and you lose.

Poet and author Kahlil Gibran said it best, "Out of suffering have emerged the strongest souls; the most massive characters are seared with scars."

Do not ignore your scars. Instead, use them to become the man you always wanted to be. At the same time, you will serve as a tremendous comfort to your frightened Inner Child.

STEP 4: TAKE CONTROL: EMPLOY RATIONAL THINKING

You have reached the point in the process where you can serve to educate and quiet the Child. After sitting and understanding the depth of his pain, you will empower yourself and control the situation.

You see, in the past, after he had been activated, you allowed the Inner Child to dictate your actions. Then, not being aware of his existence or what motivated him to run toward troubling PSBs, you gave in to compulsiveness and acted out. But now, you are empowered. He no longer runs the show; you will make that clear to him gently and caringly.

Let us go back to the example of the disappointed dad and the core negative emotions brought on by a late fee incurred for missing a payment. In Step 3, you embraced your distraught Inner Child as he recalled the painful feelings of a disapproving father.

In Step 4, you take charge by letting the Child know you will no longer follow his lead and run away from the emotional pain. Instead, you are taking charge and will rationally evaluate the current situation to determine if his pain is warranted. The conversation with him may go like this.

"I understand this event brings back feelings where you felt dad was disappointed in us," you rationalize. "But this negative event regarding the late fee was just a mistake. We all make mistakes, and I refuse to become disappointed in myself for doing so. Yes, it's annoying. I don't like having to pay extra money, but it doesn't define who I am as a person. So, it will be ok."

What you have done is take the current negative event and put it in its proper perspective, looking at it from the point-of-view of a wise mind (what is real) instead of a child-like mind (what you feel), which will always pick the easy way out of trying circumstances. Many of your decisions have been driven by child-like emotions for too long.

The time for that is over. Now, your decision-making must be based on *"what is real"* and not *"what you feel."* We will discuss this more later in this chapter. It is an especially important concept for you to comprehend and utilize daily.

You are also training your Inner Child to understand you can handle demanding situations, and he can rely on you for comfort because that is what the Child is seeking most of all – comfort. And now – unlike in the past – an adult is available to provide him that comfort.

STEP 5: MAKE THE RIGHT CHOICE

So, we come to the last step in the process. This is where we learn to make healthy choices. Remember, in the past, before you were aware the Inner Child existed, he made decisions that led you to engage in unhealthy activities. His easy solution for avoiding emotional distress caused havoc in your life and those you love. The mental and emotional anguish you have put others through is inexcusable to avoid sitting with hurtful emotions.

But you no longer need to continue to be led down the path of poor decision-making by your Inner Child. Instead, this process gives you the insight and self-discipline to make healthy decisions.

Returning to the disappointed dad and late fee, here is what your internal dialogue may sound like at this point.

"Although this situation brought up memories of how disappointed dad has been with me, I am not going to do that to myself," you declare. "Again, it was an innocent mistake. I will make a monthly reminder on my calendar to ensure it doesn't happen again. That will bring me some peace of mind. I handled that well. I am proud of myself, and that's all that matters."

What is the key difference between your Inner Child being in charge and you making the right call? Empowerment. You now have confidence and no longer need to escape and hide from your emotional pain. Instead, you distinguish it from past events and take control over how it will impact you. In this case, you have elected to learn from your mistake and make changes that will help you avoid making it again in the future. When you master this step, you are entirely in charge.

WORD OF WARNING

A potential pitfall could severely impact your ability to walk through these steps effectively, which is becoming drained. So, what does drained look like?

It is whenever you get depleted mentally, emotionally, physically, or spiritually. Becoming drained could occur due to numerous internal and external factors you face daily. In fact, it is fair to say most men walk around partially drained daily. Life comes at you hard at times, and with it comes enormous pressures. That is why you often feel extremely overwhelmed by daily circumstances.

Think about how you feel when you are tired, depressed, lonely, run-down, hopeless, or bored (to name a few). Would you say you are thinking clearly during those times? Indeed, you are not. That is because your mind and body focus on what is draining you. Therefore, you may find it more difficult to notice a negative event or process the core emotional trigger that activated your Inner Child.

When we become drained, bad things happen because your brain screams, *"stimulation, please!"*

Because you are more likely to be reactive when drained, you must be aware of your mental, emotional, physical, and spiritual states. When cognizant that you are getting depleted, you can also become more aware of lurking danger.

"Be sober-minded; be watchful. Your adversary, the devil, prowls around like a roaring lion, seeking someone to devour" Peter 5:8.

This popular Biblical verse is essential for those struggling with addiction. In our case, the lion is the temptation of problematic sexual behaviors. Being alert that danger surrounds us often, we can take the most beneficial action to prepare ourselves – practice.

What is your game plan when temptations arise? What will you do if you feel drained? These are great questions, but you cannot wait until the circumstances arise to answer them. You need to practice what actions you will take. You must determine how to stay ahead of the curve in these potentially troubling situations. If you do not, you will continue to be caught by surprise and mindlessly give in to your compulsive behaviors. **PRACTICE, PRACTICE, PRACTICE.**

For example, how do we stay alert and stay replenished? We identify potential lifelines. You can tap into these healthy resources to boost pleasant and flourishing energy. Some examples are:

- Hobbies and interests
- Reading Scripture and praying
- Spending time with good friends
- Listening or playing music
- Watching funny movies
- Playing golf, tennis, or pickleball
- Reading uplifting books
- Cooking
- Exercising
- Journaling
- Mediation
- Yoga
- Volunteer work

The list goes on and on. But it is essential to identify these resources and have them ready to engage when you become depleted mentally, emotionally, physically, or spiritually.

It also is necessary to have lifetimes that you can use immediately and more long-term. What do I mean by that? Let us say it is Tuesday afternoon, and you are at work when you start to feel physically depleted. Taking a nap is most likely not an option. Therefore, you need a lifeline to boost your energy to get you through the rest of the workday. A short-term pick-me-up may be an energy bar you keep at your desk. You need to identify both immediate and long-term lifelines for each of the four categories so that you are always prepared when feeling drained.

Remember, when you are drained, bad things happen.

STAYING AHEAD OF THE KID

Have you noticed a trend here? What you are doing is staying one step ahead of the Child. When you engage in the Inner Child Model process, you become aware of core emotional triggers and alert to negative events that bring on the triggers. At the same time, you are engaging in consistent self-reflection to determine your mental, emotional, physical, and spiritual states. By engaging in this proactive approach, you will notice your Inner Child's tantrums much earlier instead of mindlessly allowing them to play in the background and ultimately spin out of control. Your newfound alertness is a major key to managing your PSBs.

WHAT ELSE?

Along with the steps outlined above, additional aspects of recovery can ensure you effectively manage your PSBs moving forward. These include:

- Participating in Community (Group Therapy)
- Understanding Your Partner's Trauma
- Conducting a Review of Sexual History/Sexual Interests
- Identifying Your Negative Narratives
- Processing Past Trauma and/or Neglect
- Engaging in a 12-Step Program
- Understanding Healthy Sexuality
- Doing Emotional IQ Work
- Developing a Servant's Heart (being a giver, not a taker)

- Bringing Truth and Change to Every Area of Your Life
- Identifying New Interests/Passions/Hobbies

OTHER POTENTIAL STEPS

- 90-Days Abstinence
- Formal Disclosure/Polygraph
- Recovery Homework/Reading
- Medication (antidepressant if needed)

COMMUNITY

Going alone is a route littered with potholes when recovering from PSBs. As I am sure you will hear from your counselor, the lone wolf fails. Recovery is not meant to be accomplished in isolation. Let's face it, isolation has been part of the problem, so it certainly cannot be part of the solution.

Surrounding yourself with other men who have endured similar struggles accomplishes several objectives, including universality, which is the understanding that you are not suffering alone. Knowing others are dealing with similar issues and have the same worries, concerns, and struggles you face is helpful.

"I was shocked when I looked around the room and noticed these guys looked like me," said Trevor, one of my clients who dealt with pornography addiction and was reporting back after attending his first recovery meeting. *"I'm not sure what I expected, but it wasn't as frightening as I thought. On the contrary, knowing I was among other men who understood what I had been going through was comforting."*

A recovery community is also a great starting point for cultivating emotionally intimate relationships. Meeting with men and sharing your worries, fears, and concerns is the gateway to becoming emotionally connected with others. And that is a catalyst for ultimate recovery.

As I mentioned earlier, one of the most common complaints I hear from spouses and partners is their men do not know anything about emotional intimacy. Guys like us often find it challenging to engage in conversations, avoid being vulnerable, and share what troubles us. You have a better chance of hitting the Mega Million Lottery before we break down and share intimate details of our lives.

The reason is we are emotionally undeveloped. We did not receive the guidance and direction required during the initial stages of childhood development to learn how to identify and regulate our emotions, be empathic and attuned, and connect and trust others emotionally.

I refer to us as – simple men. That does not mean I think we are simpletons. It means we lack the tools necessary to engage in self-reflection and learn more about how we are hard-wired. By nature, we are not very curious, and we elect to move through life with our heads down, missing many unique and wonderful things along the way.

As discussed in an earlier chapter, emotional intimacy is a foreign concept. But to become men of integrity, we must learn to do things differently. And that requires us to lift our heads and be observant of our environment and the needs and desires of those around us.

Being vulnerable does not make us weak. However, not engaging emotionally with others makes us dead inside. It is time to start living and see what we have missed all these years. And it begins by putting our fears aside and allowing others to see the real us – warts and all.

My book, *Why Men Struggle to Love: Overcoming Relational Blind Spots,* outlines the plight of the emotionally undeveloped man.

Critical. Critical. Critical.

What I am about to write next cannot be emphasized enough and could be the deciding factor in your ability to remain sober. Let me start with this point.

We are all vulnerable.

I know you do not like to read that, but no matter how long you have been sober, there is always a risk of relapse. That could be a depressing and frightening thought, but it does not have to be. If you adhere to the following, your likelihood of relapsing will be slim to none despite your continued vulnerability.

Recovering from any addiction means you must commit to focusing on one growth activity daily to help keep you grounded. Just one activity. What could that be:

- Speaking with or spending time with a safe friend
- Calling a recovery partner/sponsor
- Surrounding yourself with family
- Reading an article or chapter of a recovery book

- Reading something that assists you in your journey of mental, emotional, or spiritual grow
- Watching an educational podcast
- Reading Scripture or other religious teachings
- Journaling
- Doing recovery work
- Volunteering
- Quiet time, self-reflection, and prayer
- Meditating

This is a partial list, and the ideas are endless. The point is to engage in one activity each day that helps you reflect on two points.

1. Although I am sober, I am still vulnerable

2. I may be vulnerable, but for today, I am in an excellent place, and my risk of relapsing is extremely low

This is where I think most men error. They take their sobriety for granted and continue with life mindlessly as they get hit left and right by the negative circumstances life throws their way. Over time, these complying, detrimental events result in men becoming drained. And you know what occurs when we are drained — bad things happen.

Men I counsel hear me say this often, "You cannot wait until you get in the trenches to determine if you are going to make a healthy decision. You must prepare yourself ahead of time for the unexpected."

Again, I cannot stress this point enough. You will be doing yourself and your loved one a great disservice if you do not commit to engaging in at least one activity daily that is focused on your mental, emotional, and spiritual growth.

INNER CHILD EXERCISES

You can use the following therapeutic techniques to train yourself to manage your Inner Child better and desensitize his core emotional triggers. These exercises should be utilized daily and must become part of your new lifestyle. If you do not commit to these practices, your Inner Child will struggle to become less reactive. It is up to you and your commitment to determine how successful you will be on this journey.

WHAT YOU FEEL VS. WHAT IS REAL

We discussed this earlier, but it is a critical component of the Inner Child Model. Many who struggle with PSBs report not thinking about anything leading up to their state of hypo-arousal. Instead, they claim to be focused on the emotions associated with their state of sexual arousal.

Whether you are mindful of your emotions or thoughts when your Inner Child is activated does not matter. What is important is for you to rise above the sexual arousal and become focused on the bigger picture:

- Why am I feeling aroused currently?
- What negative event has triggered my Inner Child?
- Am I drained mentally, emotionally, physically, or spiritually?

Once you have answered the questions, process the Inner Child's pain points (what you feel) and compare them using your wise mind (what is real). I have clients who utilize this exercise numerous times a week and report amazing success with the results.

The bottom line is you can no longer allow your Inner Child to push you toward acting out. Instead, you must slow everything down and approach your emotional discomfort differently. And that approach is one of being mature and honorable toward yourself and your loved ones.

Remember how your parents taught you to "look before you walk" when crossing the street? You must approach your PSBs similarly and "think before you act."

LETTER TO YOUR CHILD

This highly effective exercise will allow you to grow closer to your Inner Child. Everyone given this assignment asks the same question, *"What do I write?"* That is completely up to you. But know this, you have spent enough time over the past several months understanding your Inner Child and his core emotional triggers. You have uncovered faded memories that have sometimes been troubling and hurtful to recall. You have come to know many of the pain points within your Child.

Utilize that insight to determine what you want to write. Perhaps you will focus on several painful memories that have recently been recalled. Maybe you will decide to discuss and evaluate the fears that reside in your Child. Or you may elect to offer some wisdom or encouragement to help your Inner Child feel more at ease and comfortable.

The direction you take is up to you. However, the letter must focus on emotions and not just factual information. Writing a laundry list of circumstances that occurred when you were young is pointless if you do not identify the Child's pain points.

Once you have finished the letter, let it sit for a couple of days and re-read it. You most likely will have more insights you want to add. Then, reach out to a trusted friend, accountability partner, or your therapist to read the letter aloud. Encourage them to ask questions and, more importantly, check in on your emotional state as you process what you wrote. I strongly encourage you to be vulnerable with them and share your deepest emotions and thoughts.

Hopefully, this becomes a standard practice as you write to your Inner Child once or twice weekly.

LETTER FROM YOUR INNER CHILD

This exercise is a little different from the one above. This time, you are switching roles and writing to your adult self, using the voice and emotions of your Inner Child. Allow yourself to drift back to your younger self and encourage the Child to share with you his major concerns. Also, encourage him to share pain points from the past that may assist you in uncovering additional core emotional triggers.

So, here is the kicker. You are going to write this letter with your non-dominant hand. Therefore, if you write right-handed, you will draft this letter using your left hand. And vis-a-versa. Although using your non-dominant hand will make writing more challenging, do not allow this to limit the content you write. Break up the writing assignment over hours or days if that will help you to incorporate everything your Inner Child has to communicate.

Once you are done, follow the directions outlined in the previous exercise and share what you have written with someone you trust. Also, make it a practice to have your Inner Child write to you once or twice a week moving forward.

EMOTIONAL REGULATION

When your Inner Child is activated, your emotional discomfort (anxiety) will steadily heighten, increasing your risk of acting out. To counterbalance this process, you must learn to regulate your discomfort.

Emotional regulation is essential for maintaining your recovery and can be achieved in numerous ways. One of the most popular is a deep breathing exercise known as Box Breathing. It is utilized as part of U.S. Marine training. This is how the breathing exercise works.

Box Breathing is a technique where you take slow, deep

Breaths. You start by breathing in as you count to four. You then hold your breath for four seconds. Finally, you breathe out for four seconds and then hold your breath for four seconds.*

---

* https://www.healthline.com/health/box-breathing#tips

Attempt to practice this daily so that when you become emotionally deregulated, you can focus on returning to a normal emotional state.

MANAGING SEXUAL THOUGHTS/TEMPTATIONS

Do you know you can control your thoughts and temptations? Many struggling with PSBs do not think they have this capability. So, they fall victim to the same behaviors repeatedly.

Temptations often feel relentless, with no way out except to submit to them. The truth is temptations are not that powerful, they only "feel" that way. Temptations, if handled correctly, fade and eventually dissipate.

The key to making this happen is to learn to stay in the moment. When sexual thoughts, imagery, or fantasy strike, we tend to go into la-la land — just like children do. We fade, absorbed in the excitement of all that captivates our minds. The present moment and everything in it are light-years away.

We must pull ourselves out of this alluring trance and return to reality. We do this by practicing mindfulness. In this case, we start with the following:

- Memorize the core emotional triggers that impact your Inner Child and creates temptations.
- Be aware of negative events as they occur and see if they match up with your core emotional triggers. If yes, you must prepare for your Inner Child to be activated.

- At this point, identify the emotions you are experiencing and realize most of them originate with your Inner Child.

- Take notice of your anxiety level. Do you find it increasing – slowly or quickly – that indicates the Inner Child has been activated?

- Sit with the emotions you identified and feel the discomfort they cause. Can you identify circumstances in your past where you felt similar emotions? If so, feel the sadness associated with them.

- Next, you must move away from raw, child-driven emotions (What You Feel) and process them with rational thinking (What is Real). The adult has taken charge, and you have elected not to be driven by child-like emotions but instead to use your wise mind and develop healthy solutions to the circumstances at hand.

WRAPPING UP

So, we come to the final part of my proposed recovery journey – if you elect to accept it. And that is the need to maintain self-care. That includes all the basics, such as proper nutrition, restful sleep, regular exercise, etc. But adequate self-care is centrally everything we have discussed in this book, especially developing the practice of engaging in honest self-reflection to be sure you are truthful to yourself.

New York Times best-selling author Bryant McGill puts it this way "People who have had little self-reflection live life in a huge reality blind- spot."

We should never stop the process of self-exploring and should always maintain a hunger to learn about the complexities of our inner self and Inner Child. We also must seek to discover the untapped resources we can utilize to bring true purpose to our lives. Because ultimately, it is through our ability to make a difference – even if it only impacts one person – that we feel valued. I cannot begin to count the number of men I have worked with over the years who have gone on to work with other men as counselors, mentors, and recovery group leaders after learning to manage their PSBs successfully.

They have taken the pain and scars of their PSBs and turned them into something that brings hope to those who are early in the battle. That is what self-reflection can do. And when you work to implement this entire process, especially coming to know your Inner Child, you too can discover freedom from your PSBs and, more importantly, have a better appreciation of life and the absolute joy it can bring.

Successfully implementing this process takes dedication, commitment, and practice. But I know you can do it. I did it and have worked with hundreds of men who found freedom by learning to comfort their Inner Child. The keys to success are the following:

- An endless pursuit of personal insight and self-reflection
- Answering the why questions

- Slowing everything down
- Learning to sit and process emotional distress
- Generating a game plan to replenish when you are depleted
- Strengthening your emotional IQ
- Engaging in overall self-care
- Participating in community

No matter your mistakes or who you hurt or disappointed, the closing chapter of your life has not been written. This is now your opportunity to finish strong. Blessings to each of you.

REFERENCES

Armstrong, Eric. *The Nature of Sexual Addiction.* www.TreeLight.com. 2004.

Bader, Michael J. Arousal: The Secret Logic of Sexual Fantasies. St. Martin Press. 2002.

Bauman, Andrew J. *The Psychology of Porn.* Independently published. February 9, 2018.

Bradshaw, John. Homecoming: Reclaiming and Healing Your Inner Child. Bantam Books. 1990.

Carvalho, Esly Regina. Carvalho. *Healing the Folks Who Live Inside.* EMDR Treinamento e Consultoria Ltda. 2013.

Colbert, Ty. Broken Brains or Wounded Hearts. Kevco Pub. 1996.

Diamond, Stephen A., Ph.D., Psychology Today (Online Version). *Essential Secrets of Psychotherapy: The Inner Child.* June 7, 2008.

Franklin, DeVon. *The Truth About Men.* Howard Books, New York. 2018.

Hunter, M. *The Sexually Abused Man.* Vol. 1. Jossey-Bass Pub. 1990.

Martino, Anthony. The Inconsequential Child: Overcoming Emotional Neglect. Vangelo Media. 2015.

O'Malley, Mary. What's in the Way Is the Way: A Practical Guide for Waking Up to Life. True Sounds, Boulder, CO. 2016.

Price, Donald, Ph.D. Inner Child Work: What is Really Happening. Dissociation. Vol. IX, No. 1, March 1996.

Price, Matt. Inner Child: Find Your True Self, Discover Your Inner Child, and Embrace the Fun in Life. 2014, Self-published.

Secunda, Victoria. When You and Your Mother Can't Be Friends: Resolving the Most Complicated Relationship of Your Life. Delta. 2009.

Solomon, Stacey M. *Childhood Loneliness: Implications and Intervention Considerations for Family Therapists.* The Family Journal: Counseling and Therapy for Couples and Families. April 2000.

Skinner, Kevin B. Ph.D. Treating Pornography Addiction: The Essential Tools for Recovery. Growth Climate Inc. Provo, Utah. 2005.

Stringer, Jay. Unwanted. How Sexual Brokenness Reveals Our Way to Healing. NavPress. 2018.

Susskind, Andrew. *It's Not About the Sex.* Central Recovery Press. 2019.

Van Der Kolk, Bessel, M.D. The Body Keeps the Score: Brain, Mind, and Body in the Healing of Trauma. Penguin Books. 2015.

Webb, Jonice. *Running on Empty.* Morgan James Publishing. 2016.

Yerkovich, M. Yerkovich, K. *How We Love: Expanded Edition.* WaterBrook Publishing. 2017.

ABOUT THE AUTHOR

Eddie Capparucci, Ph.D. LPC, C-CSAS

 Dr. Eddie Capparucci is a licensed counselor certified in treating Problematic Sexual Behaviors. He and his wife, Teri, have a private practice working with men struggling with sex and pornography and their wives dealing with betrayal trauma.

He created the Inner Child Model™ for treating Problematic Sexual Behaviors. He has worked with professional athletes among his many clients, including NFL and MLB players and television personalities. He sits on the board of Certified Sex Addiction Specialists International, an organization committed to training counselors, coaches, and church leaders.

He is the administrator of the websites MenAgainstPorn.org and SexuallyPureMen.com. He has also written for Covenant Eyes, KingdomWorks, XXXChurch, Live Free, and Seeking Integrity. Over the years, he has spoken to numerous organizations regarding the harmful impact porn has on individuals, relationships, and society.

He is also the author of the books Why Men Struggle to Love: Overcoming Relational Blind Spots, Understanding Your Inner Child and Overcoming Addiction, and Removing Your Shame Label: Learning to Break From Shame and Feel God's Love.

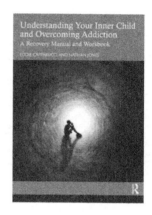

CLINICIAN CERTIFICATION PROGRAM

If you are a counselor, social worker, coach, or pastor who sees value in the Inner Child Model and how it can help those struggling with various Problematic Sexual Behaviors and other mental health

disorders, I invite you to become a certified Inner Child Model™ clinician.

Since the launch of *Going Deeper: How the Inner Child Impacts Your Sexual Addiction*, potential clients worldwide have sought counseling and coaching services using this new treatment approach. Unfortunately, only a few clinicians are trained in this process, so potential clients cannot obtain the value this program offers. So, we are offering this special certification to those who want to bring the Inner Child Model into their practice.

By completing this seven-course program, you will not only be prepared to introduce the Inner Child Model to your clients but also:

- Will be certified in the Inner Child Model by Pure Life Academy, part of Be Broken Ministry
- Become a member of the Inner Child Model Referral Network
- Have your contact information added to the www.innerchild-sexaddiction.com website

To learn more and to enroll in the Inner Child Model training program, go to:
https://www.purelifeacademy.org/bundles/ictc

GOING DEEPER ONLINE COURSE

This 12-part video series will empower you by teaching you how to stay one step ahead of your Problematic Sexual Behaviors and your Inner Child.

The course provides additional insights into managing your disorder and gives you the newfound capability to make healthy decisions.

Conducted by Dr. Capparucci, you will go deeper in your recovery journey as you learn more about the reasons why you think, feel, and act the way you do.

- This course you will assist you in:
- Generating on-going self-reflection
- Reducing compulsiveness
- Increasing mindfulness
- Better understanding your emotions
- Achieving and maintaining your sobriety

The course has been priced to assist those who cannot afford on-going therapy sessions. For less than the price of 3 therapy sessions you receive a comprehensive overview of the Inner Child Model™ and how it applies to your situation.

You can learn more by visiting www.innerchild-sexaddiction.com

Printed in Great Britain
by Amazon

44299399R00185